JUST AS LONG AS I'M RIDING UP FRONT

More stories I couldn't tell while I was a pastor

JUST AS LONG AS I'M RIDING UP FRONT

Bruce McIver

WORD PUBLISHING
Dallas · London · Vancouver · Melbourne

Library of Congress Cataloging-in-Publication Data

McIver, Bruce.
Just as long as I'm riding up front: more stories I couldn't tell while I was a pastor/Bruce McIver.
p. cm.
ISBN 0–8499–3597–0
1. Christian life—humor. 2. Christian life—Anecdotes. 3. McIver, Bruce. 4. American wit and humor. I. Title.
BV4517.M35 1995
286'.1'092—dc20
[B] 94–44566
CIP

7 8 9 LBM 7 6 5 4 3

Printed in the United States of America

To Lawanna,
Kathie, Shannon, and Renie—
the four most important women in my life
who have loved me, encouraged me, laughed with me
and helped me to laugh at myself—
thanks.

Acknowledgments

Interestingly, this page—at the very beginning of the book—is the one I wrote last. I waited 'til the end because of continuing gratitude for those special people who have helped me right up to the last moment.

Lawanna—wife, friend, and joyful companion for thirty-five years—has been a constant source of encouragement. She has read every paragraph in this book, offering constructive criticism and positive suggestions. She's a gift to me and I can't imagine life without her.

Daughters Shannon Allen and Renie McCarthy have been most supportive. Shannon and Renie jogged my memory and helped me fill in some of the blanks as I recalled these stories. Unfortunately, in the process they told me a few things about their younger days I wasn't expecting to know—now or ever! Happily, time has a way of making life more mellow, and more forgiving. Besides, I'm not about to get upset now with the mothers of my three grandchildren—Emily, Ali, and John-John.

Oldest daughter Kathie, now a college English teacher, has read and edited most of these stories with a fine, sharp pencil. I had hoped that she might show her old father some leniency, but she has been tough on me as she would be on a freshman student taking one of her courses in composition. I sometimes have the strange feeling that she thinks it's "payback" time!

Barbara Jenkins, a best-selling author and a dear friend, has been a primary encourager from the beginning. Thanks.

Thirty-six years ago I became the pastor of the Wilshire Baptist Church in Dallas. For thirty years and one month we walked together, worshiped together, wept together, and laughed together. It was a great journey, and no retired pastor ever felt more gratitude than I do. Today the pastor, George Mason, is my pastor, and he and the members of Wilshire are the best friends Lawanna and I could have. We are very fortunate and would like to thank our Wilshire family for their prayers and love.

A special word of thanks to the people who are a part of these stories. In many cases they have laughed with me before the stories were ever written down. Now, they have graciously freed me up and given me permission to use their names in sharing their experiences. In a few cases, however, the names were changed—to protect *me!*

Finally, my gratitude to Joey Paul, vice president, Word Publishing, Inc., and to Alyse Lounsberry, editor at Word, for their encouragement, suggestions, and—most of all—patience.

Contents

Introduction

On a recent visit to Dallas, four-year-old granddaughters Emily and Ali raced across the den, climbed up in my lap, and snuggled close.

"Tell me a story, 'Goose,'" Emily said excitedly as she put her arm around my neck.

"Yeah, 'Bwoose,'" Ali giggled, "tell us about the time when you were a little boy and the goat butted you off the porch."

Two-year-old John-John, content to let his sister and cousin do most of the talking, nodded his head, grinned, and climbed on up beside his sisters.

I smiled and wrapped all three of them up in my arms, grateful that after nearly three-score and ten years and two heart surgeries, I was still around to bask in the warmth of this moment. I didn't even mind that Ali had tagged me "Bwoose" or that Emily called me "Goose," although I wondered at times if "Father Goose" or "Granddaddy Goose" wouldn't have sounded a little better. But I had learned early on that when your grandchildren name you, you're branded for life.

So I told them about my pet goat that didn't act like a pet. I told them about my first little dog, Trixie, and how she yelped in excitement each day when I came home from school; I told them about little rabbits that played in our yard and squirrels that gathered and hid nuts in the woods; I told them about my own Grandpa Moody and how I loved to ride his horse, Roberta. I told them all these stories—along with embarrassing experiences I had at weddings that went awry, near-drownings at baptisms, getting lost on the way to cemeteries, and losing my way through sermons. Of course, they giggled with glee, as little children do.

I have tried to tell them about God—how He loves and cares for them—through simple, everyday stories.

Simple stories to explain the profound things of life? Everyday stories to shed light on eternal truths?

Admittedly, I wondered at times whether this was really possible—until I remembered some of the words of the One who came to give us life: "Look at the birds . . . . ;" "consider the lilies of the fields . . . ;" and "a man had two sons." Finally, I pondered, "except ye be as a little child . . . ."

Today, I believe these simple stories of His are called "parables."

So, pull up a chair, and let me tell you a story.

"Once upon a time . . . ."

1

Lost—On the Way to "RIP"

The memorial service concluded at the church and the funeral director invited me to ride with him to the cemetery.

"You're new in the city," he said graciously, "and this will give us an opportunity to get to know one another better. "Besides," he added, "the burial is in a small private cemetery—one of the last in Dallas—and you might have some trouble finding your way back to the church."

"That sounds like a good idea," I replied. "I'll enjoy visiting with you, and I'm still trying to learn my way around this city. Just let me pick up my Bible and my notes and I'll be with you in a second."

"Take your time," he answered with ease. "It will take a few minutes for us to gather up the flowers and see that the family and friends are in their cars. We'll also have to wait until the motorcycle escorts give us the signal to start."

This man is smooth, I thought. *He's got a dozen things on his mind; yet he's the essence of efficiency. He exudes a quiet, calming confidence. And, along with all this, he's taking time to look after my needs*. I was impressed.

"Oh, by the way," he added as he walked away, "we're a little short of help today. This is our fourth service, so I'll be driving the funeral coach myself." Then he looked around to make sure that he was not being overheard, and whispered, "Hope you don't mind riding in a hearse."

"Not at all," I responded in the same whispered tones, "*just as long as I'm riding up front.*"

We smiled politely at each other, realizing that it would not be appropriate to laugh openly—not even to grin.

Less than ten minutes later the escorts turned on the flashing signal lights of their motorcycles and we eased out of the church parking lot and headed north on Abrams Road. The director kept one eye on the road ahead, and the other on the rearview mirror, checking to be sure that the thirty cars in the funeral procession were moving at an orderly pace.

As we turned right off Abrams and headed east on Northwest Highway my new friend reached for a piece of paper on the seat between us. He studied it for a minute, muttering to himself and nodding his head.

"Looks fine," he said, "I had the folks in the office draw me a map to the cemetery. We'll turn right again down here on Buckner, pass by White Rock Lake on the right, and move on through the Casa Linda area. Did you know that it's twelve miles around the lake, and did you know that Casa Linda is one of the oldest shopping centers in Dallas?"

I didn't, but I was fascinated by his easy, animated travelogue.

"And from Casa Linda we go to east to . . ." His voice trailed off as he glanced again into the rearview mirror. "No need to worry about directions now," he added as he laid the hand-drawn map down. "My biggest concern at the moment is that all those cars make it safely through that busy intersection back there."

They did, and the motorcycle escorts zoomed on ahead to clear the way at the next crowded crossing.

We continued east, making turns here and there that had me completely confused. The escorts appeared confused also. From time to time they glided up next to the hearse with question marks on their faces. The director smiled through the window at them, picked up the map and instructions from the seat, and gave them an affirming nod to move on ahead. With this reassurance they revved their engines and roared on to the next intersection. It was a good feeling to know that the funeral director had matters so well under control.

And, it was good to talk. We discussed churches, city leaders, and sports. Mostly sports. We shared thoughts about the Dallas Texans, the AFL football team that was the talk of the town. I told him proudly that five or six of the players, including the quarterback, were members of the church that I pastored. We also discussed briefly the "new kids on the block," the Dallas Cowboys. I mentioned that I had gone to a Cowboy game recently and the attendance was less than 10,000. He shook his head, and both of us wondered aloud if the Cowboys and their new coach, Tom Landry, would make it in Dallas—or anywhere else. We were totally absorbed in our speculations—so much so that we failed to realize that by now we were well beyond the city limits of Dallas . . . moving slowly through the suburbs of Mesquite . . . away from busy intersections . . . traveling along some obscure farm-to-market road. . . .

LOST, BUT STILL LEADING

Lost. Completely lost.

The funeral director, his furrowed brow beaded with perspiration, drove nervously with one hand and clutched the now-crumpled map in the other. The procession had slowed to a crawl and the escorts lingered further behind. It was obvious that they didn't want to be identified as the "leaders" of this misdirected caravan. The director didn't say a word; he just glanced repeatedly at the map, then at the farmland surrounding us. I turned and looked back over my shoulder. Thirty cars were still following us. We didn't know where we were, or where we were going, but at least we hadn't *lost* anybody! The meandering procession had remained in tact, the drivers of all thirty vehicles looking to *us* for leadership!

Finally, the director spoke with hesitation. "Bruce," he said, "I think we've missed a road, or maybe several of them. We're already beyond the Mesquite city limits. We've got to turn around and go back."

I was a young pastor and had never considered the hazards of trying to turn a hearse around in the middle of an asphalt, two-lane country road. And how do you communicate your intentions to thirty bewildered drivers behind you? But, as is true with most funeral directors, this man was very resourceful. That's why they gave him the title "director."

We topped a hill at a snail's pace and spotted on the right, immediately before us, a dilapidated "filling station" with two lonely-looking gasoline pumps. The once-white paint on the building had long since peeled, and three or four old cars ringed an area designated: "GARAGE—Mechanic on Duty." Potholes, filled with water from recent rains, punctuated the graveled driveway. An old white icebox, with "COLD DRINKS" hand-lettered on it, leaned to the left of the screen-door entrance.

At the first crunching sounds of tires on gravel and the sloshing of wheels in water holes the lone attendant sitting on a crate next to the icebox, half asleep, yawned and stood. Then without bothering to look up, he moved lazily toward the pumps. In one motion he slowly lifted a hose with one hand and pushed the lever to the "on" position with the other. He then waited for his customers to stop.

We were his first "customers"—the funeral director, the pastor, and the deceased—all in the lead car. But we didn't stop. Without saying a word, the director steered the long hearse around a pothole, skillfully avoided the ice box, made a sharp U-turn, and headed back toward Dallas. Other "customers," including the motorcycle escorts—now at the rear of the procession—obediently followed their leader.

I nodded and waved politely at the startled attendant as we maneuvered our way through his driveway. After we made our

U-turn, I looked back over my left shoulder and could see him standing there—confused, bewildered, and holding a limp, dangling gasoline hose with his right hand.

I never knew the name of the gasoline attendant but I could tell he was a gentleman. By the time we had topped the hill, going back in the opposite direction, he had removed his floppy cap with his other hand, and in a gesture of respect, he had placed it over his heart. I was told later that he held that position while all thirty cars circled through his place of business.

Forty-five minutes later, after numerous other turns, we found the small, private cemetery. I read a passage of Scripture, led in prayer, spoke to the family, and joined the director as we headed back west toward the church. The conversation on the way back was sparse. Even my mention of rumors of the possible move of the Dallas Texans to Kansas City didn't seem to excite the dour-faced funeral director. Instead, he kept looking at his watch and mumbling something about "another service."

When we reached the church parking lot I thanked him, shook his hand, and said the wrong thing: "Maybe we can do this again someday."

He smiled weakly, made no reply, and drove off.

I watched him exit the church parking lot and made a simple decision: I refuse to ride in a hearse again—until they put me in the back of it!

"THAT'S WHAT I DREAD ABOUT DYING!"

"Who cares who the speaker is?" Or, "who cares about the program?" "I'm just interested in Miss Julia's pies."

Those were the attitudes of most of the members of the Kiwanis Club in San Marcos, Texas as they gathered weekly in the early '50s at Julia's Tearoom. Miss Julia, showing unusual entrepreneurial skills, had taken a stately old antebellum house on San Antonio Street, renovated it, and turned it into one of the finest eating establishments in the area. Her business skills, coupled with her culinary abilities, made her tearoom a favorite gathering place for luncheons.

THURSDAY–MEN STILL BOYS

But on Thursdays the tearoom was off-limits for everybody but the Kiwanians. As this day rolled around each week the civic club members lined up early, waiting for the doors to open. It was an occasion for unscheduled and uninhibited fellowship. The men laughed loudly and called out greetings to one another, punctuating their salutations with hearty handshakes and slaps on the back. Some entered into exciting discussions on what the entree of the day would be, and a few took delight in making small bets on the height of the meringue atop Miss Julia's lemon pies.

Thursday was a day in San Marcos when grown men became children again—for a couple of hours.

Promptly at twelve o'clock the doors opened and university professors, professional businessmen, salesmen, representatives of the medical field, and hourly laborers rushed in like kids playing "musical chairs." They scrambled for the best tables—meaning, of course, the tables they predicted would be the first served that day. It was just another part of the weekly game.

And it was great fun—a brief reprieve from the daily routines of lecturing to sleepy students, making rounds at the community hospital, attending committee meetings, promoting sales, and pushing levers and switches on the job. Everybody participated.

Everybody except Roger Shelton.

Roger was a "good old boy," well-liked by the rest of the members of the club, but he was a quiet person—a loner. He would usually arrive late for the meetings, after all the jostling and the backslapping and the scrambling for tables had subsided. He would survey the group and then would slip to an isolated table in a less crowded part of the room. This served two purposes: It kept him from having to talk with people about things he wasn't interested in, and it afforded him the opportunity to slip out of the room if the program didn't appeal to him. He often took advantage of this option.

Roger was a paradox. Deep down inside he seemed to care for people but, like a lone Texan on the prairie, he sought solitude. He contributed to the civic projects sponsored by the club, but he did it quietly—without fanfare. He wasn't much of a talker but, when necessary, he could cut through tangled discussions, get to the heart of the matter, and offer the solution in a terse, straightforward sentence.

When most of the members had gathered, with or without Roger, the president would tap a fork or a knife lightly on the side of a glass in an effort to bring the meeting to order. If this didn't work, others at the head table would help him by tapping on their glasses also. And, if the crowd continued to talk, some uninhibited, self-appointed member would shout out above the noise, "Okay, everybody *shut up!*" No one ever seemed to take offense at being told to "shut up." This, too, was part of the game.

When the noise level had muffled to snickers, the president of the club asked someone to pray or, as he usually put it, to "lead the invocation." Because I was a Bible Instructor at Southwest Texas State University, I was often included in these requests. I learned quickly that grown men—even with Ph.D.s—have limited attention spans when caught up in savoring the aroma of Miss Julia's cooking. So, the principle was simple: the shorter the prayer, the greater the gratitude.

After the brief prayer came the pledge of allegiance, with someone at every table inevitably forgetting the words and mumbling his way to the finish. Finally, before the food could be touched, we would sing a stanza of "God Bless America." Two bars from the end of the song the metal chairs would begin to clang as hungry Kiwanians prepared to "dive in."

When the meal was finished it was time for the program. Topics of these varied with the seasons, the community emphases, the special projects sponsored by the club, and the availability of politicians and others who were "turned on" by podiums and lecterns.

On one occasion a local quartet was invited to sing. This foursome consisted of college professors, all with their Ph.D.s—in subjects other than music! But they enjoyed harmonizing in barbershop-style.

They were good—so good that they were often asked to sing at functions at the university and in the community.

And . . . at the funeral home.

Willard Pennington, a congenial civic leader in San Marcos, owned Pennington's Funeral Home located three blocks down the hill from the college. When a family had no specific requests concerning music for a funeral service, Willard would recommend his four college professors. They could leave the campus, dash down the hill, sing two songs, slip out the back door of the funeral home, and never even miss a class. Besides, a few extra dollars in the early '50s went a long way to supplement the meager salaries earned by college teachers. They sang so often for Willard that they were dubbed the "Funeral Quartet."

THE FUNERAL QUARTET . . . SINGS 'EM QUIET

So on this Thursday, after a glowing introduction, the Funeral Quartet began to sing their first number, "Fairest Lord Jesus."

I'm not sure what happened, but I think the person singing the lead pitched it in the wrong key. It was all downhill from there. Terrible. Never has "Fairest Lord Jesus" ever been so rendered—or should I say "rended." What I mean is, "torn apart." The longer they sang, the worse they got. The Kiwanians in attendance bowed their heads (to keep from having to look anyone in the eye), scratched their eyebrows (to give the appearance of prayerful concern), coughed and cleared their throats (to keep from snickering), and lifted cups of cold coffee to their lips (just to have something to do). It was so bad that most people would have given all they had in their pockets to be able to slip out a rear door, or to be carried out! It really didn't seem to matter which!

When the Funeral Quartet sang the last note, still off-key, they sat down. Unfortunately, there was no curtain separating them from the audience like there was at Pennington's Funeral Home. And there was no back door. Escape was impossible, so they just stared blankly, ignoring the generous pieces of lemon pie left for them at their places around the table. No one reached for his fork. Even the promise of savoring Miss Julia's pie couldn't redeem this situation!

Silence. Not a word was spoken. Even the president was speechless.

Embarrassment and disaster had struck the club.

Then a voice cut through the awkward silence. To everybody's amazement it was the drawling, raspy voice of Roger Shelton. He was still with us. The Funeral Quartet had so paralyzed him that he had been unable to slip out his favorite exit.

So, still seated in his chair, he observed loudly and clearly:

"You know, that's what I *dread* about dying!"

The Kiwanians, it seemed, thought Roger had summed their sentiments up nicely. Everyone broke up laughing.

THE DAY NO ONE LAUGHED

November 22, 1963.

It was a beautiful day in the city of Dallas—just the kind I enjoyed most.

The temperature was 76 degrees and there wasn't a cloud in the sky. Most of the leaves on the trees had changed colors, curled at the edges, and fallen gently to the ground. A few hung on tenaciously as though they were challenging the first "blue norther" that would sweep down from the Rockies, across the Panhandle, and through our city, sometimes plunging temperatures down as much as 40 or 50 degrees in a few hours. The norther would eventually come, and every leaf would finally fall . . . but not today. This was a special day for Dallas.

The thirty-fifth president of the United States, John Fitzgerald Kennedy, was coming to town for a brief visit. Accompanying him on the hasty tour of four Texas cities—San Antonio, Houston, Fort Worth, and Dallas—were his beautiful wife, Jacqueline, Texas Governor and Mrs. John Connally, Vice President and Mrs. Lyndon Johnson, Senator Ralph Yarborough, and other dignitaries of the Democratic Party. The trip was designed to mend fences among Democratic party leaders in Texas and to display unity in elections scheduled for 1964.

FATEFUL DECISION

"The president is scheduled to land at Love Field just before noon," Lawanna said. "Let's call Mary and Frank Wilson and see if they can keep Shannon and Renie for a couple of hours so we can go out and see him."

Lawanna is a "now" person, a celebrative spirit, a "don't-dare-miss-this-experience" kind of individual. I'm more the "wait and see," "let's think about it," "are you sure?" type.

I pondered her suggestion, thought of unfinished sermons, and mumbled something about Sunday coming in two days.

"Look," she urged impatiently, "this is supposed to be your day off from church activities; and we haven't had a lot of time together because of your schedule; and it really is the *president himself* who's coming to town." Then she added with a hint of a smile, "You tell the people to pray for our leaders; it might also help for you to go see them."

That did it. We called the Wilsons, who loved to play grandparents, listened to the excitement in their voices, and delivered Renie and Shannon, ages one and two, to their house. Kathie, our oldest, was in the sixth grade at Dan D. Rogers Elementary School.

"Now, you folks take your time about getting back," Mary said in an assuring tone. "We'll take good care of them." Frank, affectionately called "Gi-Gi" by the girls, beamed. Everybody was happy—Mary, "Gi-Gi," Shannon, Renie, and Lawanna. And in spite of my pastoral "oughtness" about sermons and visits, I was happy too. Lawanna was right—again. It was a good day, and we were on our way to welcome the President of the United States to Dallas.

We turned left on Mockingbird Lane and drove west . . . by the historic Dr. Pepper plant . . . across Central Expressway . . . alongside Southern Methodist University . . . through Highland Park . . . and to the entrance of Love Field. A large crowd had already gathered and cheering people were waving hastily prepared banners and signs—"Welcome to Dallas J.F.K," "Welcome Jack and Jackie to Big D," and "Welcome Mr. President." There was a festive mood as the well-mannered crowd of several hundred quickly grew into a crush of thousands. Lawanna and I parked the car and inched our way through the mob of people to the chain fence that separated the spectators from the airport runways.

Enthusiastic chatter was punctuated with eager glances toward the westward skies over Fort Worth, thirty miles away. Adults were like excited children, each anticipating the sight of Air Force One and each hoping to be the first to spot it.

At 11:37 the wheels of the huge, majestic, blue and white presidential jet touched down amid the cheers of the throng that had gathered. President and Mrs. Kennedy stepped through the door, waved to the crowd, moved down the steps, and shook hands with local civic leaders and politicians. Radiant Mrs. Kennedy, wearing a stylish hot pink suit and a smart black pillbox hat, was presented a large bouquet of red roses. She pushed her dark hair from her face, smiled, and waved in the direction of the admiring crowd. Then she took her place beside the president in the waiting car. Riding along with the Kennedys in the open presidential limousine were Governor and Mrs. Connally.

At 11:50 the motorcade, escorted by the Dallas Police Department's new black and white '63 Ford Galaxies and a dozen Harley Davidson motorcycles, slowly began the winding journey that would lead them through downtown Dallas and on to the Trade Mart where the president was scheduled to speak. As Lawanna and I walked to our car, I said, "I'm glad we did this. It's a lot better than watching a re-run of it on the television news tonight."

Traffic out of Love Field was congested, with cars inching along bumper to bumper, but no one seemed to be in a hurry. Individuals and families were still basking in the warmth they had just experienced in personally greeting the president and his entourage.

"Let's take the back streets," I suggested to Lawanna as we listened to the radio announcers give progress reports on the motorcade. "Gordon Abbott's barbershop is on Oak Lawn Street just a few blocks from here. I can get a quick haircut there while the traffic clears out." Gordon was a deacon in the church that I pastored, a good friend and an excellent barber.

THE PRESIDENT IS SHOT

I parked the car in front of Gordon's shop and reached to turn off the ignition but before I could, there was an awkward pause in the flow of communication—an interruption—as a second radio announcer broke in and said breathlessly, "A report . . . three shots . . . unconfirmed . . . three shots fired at President Kennedy's motorcade today in downtown Dallas. . . ."

Lawanna and I sat in stunned disbelief, straining to hear words like "correction" . . . "mistake" . . . "rumor". . . . But words like those were never spoken. Instead, we heard terms, now familiar to the world, like "Elm Street" . . . "Book Depository" . . . "triple underpass" . . . "grassy knoll". . . "Parkland Hospital" . . . Bits of sketchy information were punctuated by periods of silence—haunting silence—as stunned reporters and announcers scrambled for additional details.

The events that followed are a blur. Lawanna and I leaped out of the car and ran over to the barbershop. Inside Gordon, the other barbers, and the customers were all huddled around a small radio. Their world, like most of the rest of our worlds, had come to a halt, frozen in time and paralyzed by the hesitant, troubled voices of reporters. I don't remember if I ever got a haircut that day; I do remember the anguish I felt in my heart—and in the pit of my stomach.

We left Gordon's place hurriedly and drove quickly to the Wilsons, arriving just in time to hear Walter Cronkite—voice breaking, struggling to frame the words—announce "President Kennedy died . . . Parkland Hospital . . . 12:39 . . . today. . . ."

It was time to go home to our babies . . . time to wait for Kathie to get out of school . . . time to try to explain to her what we could not understand . . . time to be brave like mature adults . . . time to weep like little children.

On Saturday morning, after a sleepless night, I got up, dressed quietly, slipped out the door, and drove slowly toward the church. Strange. The offices were not open on Saturday, but I wanted to be alone. I didn't want to be pastor to anyone on this day. I didn't want to think about sermons, or budgets, or committees, or anything. I just wanted to be alone. When I arrived the other members of the staff were already there. We discovered that each of us had wanted the same thing: to be alone . . . together.

ALONE . . . TOGETHER

We sat together in an isolated room, shared our feelings and concerns, prayed, and wept. We also talked about church members and other friends who were caught up personally in the tragedy: two surgeons—members of our church—who were on the staff at Parkland; nurses who worked in the trauma room; a dear friend who was chief of chaplains at the hospital; policemen and civic leaders who were seeking answers and struggling for solutions; and thousands of people across the city who, like us, wanted to be alone . . . together.

"Let's have a prayer meeting here at the church tonight," someone suggested. "No program, no special music, and no sermon. Just give the people a chance to pray together and share their concerns."

There was no time for newspaper or radio announcements. The staff called some deacons, and the deacons called some teachers and committee members, and they in turn called their friends.

At seven o'clock Saturday evening over four hundred people crowded body-to-body into our chapel. I read a brief passage of Scripture from the Old Testament: "If my people, who are called by my name, will humble themselves and pray and seek my face and turn from their wicked ways, then will I hear from heaven and will forgive their sin and will heal their land" (2 Chron. 7:14 NIV).

"I have nothing else to add to this," I told the people. "You're invited to remain seated, stand, or kneel—as you wish—and pray. Feel free to pray silently or aloud."

Scores of people knelt right where they were in the aisles; others remained in their seats, bending forward with their heads resting on the pew in front of them; some stood in the back and in the foyer, leaning their bodies against the wall.

For nearly an hour there was silence, broken only by the gentle sounds of soft weeping and the whispers of burdened petitions: "O God . . . forgive . . . bless . . . guide . . . ."

When I sensed that the time was right, I stood and said simply, "Amen."

Those who had gathered quietly stood to their feet and walked out without a word.

They had been alone . . . together . . . with God.

THEN CAME SUNDAY

Sunday morning an estimated 500,000 people gathered for worship in the churches in Dallas. Overflow crowds attended each of the services at Wilshire that day.

What does a minister say to a congregation in grief? I'm not sure. I never have been sure. And, I wouldn't have remembered what I said that day—November 24, 1963—had I not found my sermon notes one day many years later as I was cleaning out some file cabinets in the garage:

> "There is no need to recount the tragic details. We are all too well aware of what has happened in our city and in our nation. We are still in a daze, a state of shock, a sense of nightmare—thinking that soon we will wake up. Slowly, the awful reality closes in upon us. It is no nightmare. We are awake. Custom does not dictate it, but we would like to sit down in sackcloth and ashes and weep our hearts out. If our city had a wailing wall like Jerusalem of old, we would lean against it and weep."
>
> "We come to this service with remorse, and repentance, and (dare I say it?) Thanksgiving. Is this the epitome of irreverence? Is this pious talk? Yet, I am reminded that the very spirit of Thanksgiving is born in suffering, trial, and adversity. The writer of Ecclesiastes said, 'In the day of prosperity be joyful; but in the day of adversity consider . . .' (Eccles. 7:14 KJV). This is a good time on the eve of Thanksgiving to stop and consider . . . that . . . out

> of the depths of this tragedy perhaps good can come. Pray God that it shall."
>
> "We will do what we must—in spite of obstacles and dangers and pressures. And, with God's help, through our remorse and repentance, blended with a spirit of thanksgiving, we will try to build a better city and a better nation. This is the essence of Christian courage."

Just before the benediction, as we prepared to leave the worship service, one of the ushers walked down the aisle and handed me a note. I glanced at it and with a trembling voice read it out loud to the congregation: "Lee Harvey Oswald was just killed at the police station."

I managed some kind of brief closing prayer, and the people filed out wordlessly. There were no back slappings or light-hearted greetings in the aisles or hallways. No "good sermon, Pastor," and no "how 'bout those Dallas Cowboys?" Nor did anyone say, "Have a nice Thanksgiving holiday." The people walked out in stunned silence.

Monday was declared a day of mourning by the now thirty-sixth president of the United States. Schools closed, businesses shut down, office buildings stood dark and vacant, the streets were empty as people stayed home, glued to their television sets, watching every facet of the memorial service. When the day was over we were physically and emotionally drained.

WE MUST GO ON

That was thirty years ago.

Kathie now teaches composition and literature courses to college students who were not yet born in 1963. Renie and Shannon are married and have children the ages they were thirty years ago. Lawanna and I are grandparents, and I have retired from pastoring. Mary Wilson is with the Lord, and "Gi-Gi" is still our special friend. Had John Fitzgerald Kennedy lived, he would be seventy-six today. He died at forty-six.

"Hail to the Chief" has been played for seven other presidents since that fateful November day in Dallas.

So, life goes on. The grieving—which knows no partisan politics—eventually subsides, although at times it returns . . . unexpectedly . . . and without invitation.

It lingers for a moment, and then we get on with life and "do what we must . . . with God's help."

2

Old Folks at Home

Years ago . . .

Ethel and Jake, newcomers to Dallas, attended worship services at Wilshire one Sunday morning. Following the service they lingered to introduce themselves to me and to visit briefly.

"We're looking for a church home here in the city, and we like what we see at Wilshire," Ethel said warmly as she shook my hand. Jake stood in the background and silently nodded his head.

"I'm grateful," I responded with a smile while breathing a silent sigh of relief that we had at least passed the first test. I knew from experience that there were other tests we'd have to pass if Ethel and Jake joined our church. These often included the number of parking spaces, the length of services, the comfort of the pews, the kind of music and the loudness of the organ, the friendliness of the congregation, and the preparation and varieties of foods served each Wednesday evening at the "fellowship dinners."

"Would it be possible for you to drop by our house later this week?" Ethel continued. "This will help us get to know each other better and will give us the chance to ask you some questions about the church. Jake and I would appreciate that very much, wouldn't we Jake?"

Jake nodded.

JAKE'S CURIOUS ABSENCE

"You just call us, Pastor, and let us know when it's convenient for you to drop by," Ethel glowed as she shook my hand a second time. "We'll be mighty glad to see you."

Then she turned and walked away. Jake followed her.

The visit was made and apparently most of their, or her, questions were answered adequately, for they joined the church the next Sunday. Both were regular in their attendance for several weeks, and then Jake became less and less involved.

"How's Jake?" I would ask Ethel.

"Oh, he's fine. This has been a difficult week at work for him, and he's worn out;" or, "he's not feeling well today;" or, "something came up unexpectedly." Ethel would always have an answer like one of these readily available, anytime I questioned her about Jake's absence.

Then one day I received an urgent telephone call. "Something's wrong, seriously wrong with Jake," Ethel cried. "He's in the hospital now and they plan to operate in a couple of hours. They say it's an emergency and has to be done. I . . . we . . . need you. Can you come to the hospital immediately?"

"Of course I can, Ethel. I'm on my way."

By the time I reached the hospital most of the relatives had already gathered. They filled Jake's room and overflowed into the corridors. Concern, accentuated by tears, was written across their faces.

"The doctors say they've found a mass, Pastor—a huge mass in his intestines. They say they'll be taking him to surgery in fifteen minutes. Please pray for him," Ethel pleaded as she reached down and took Jake by the hand. I could tell by the glazed look in his eyes that he had already received his pre-operation injection, sometimes called the "happy shot," or the "don't care shot." Poor Jake didn't look happy, but neither did he seem to care. The shot was partially working, at least.

I took Ethel by one hand and Jake by the other. Relatives crowded back into the room and I prayed briefly for Jake, for the surgeon, and for the entire family. When I finished, Ethel wept, the relatives hugged each other, and Jake snored. The "happy shot" had done its work.

Normally after having prayer with the patient and the family, I would leave to make other hospital calls or perform other pastoral duties. I would usually check with the family either during the surgery or after the operation. This time, however, I had a feeling that I needed to stick around. Ethel seemed emotionally depleted and everyone was concerned about that mass in Jake's intestines.

So I lingered. Relatives paired off or sat in small groupings, drinking coffee and struggling for encouraging words to say to one another. One older man identified himself as Jake's cousin and invited me to walk down the hall with him. As we slowly moved out of the traffic and away from the conversations, he spoke softly.

JAKE PICKS BEER

"Sad about Jake, isn't it?"

"Could be serious," I whispered.

"Sad about Jake and Ethel too," he added.

"Sad? What do you mean?"

"You don't know?"

"I have no idea what you're talking about," I replied in confusion.

"Preacher, Jake likes his beer."

"Yes?" I responded, sensing there was more to the story.

"Well, Ethel gave him an ultimatum. Told Jake, 'it's me or beer.'"

"What happened?" I asked innocently.

"Jake chose beer and moved out. Hasn't been home in over a month. Don't know where he's been living, but he's sure not been with Ethel."

Slowly the picture was coming into focus for me. That's why I hadn't seen Jake in church, and that's why Ethel had been making excuses for his absence. Apparently he had allowed her to take the initiative, be aggressive, and make all the decisions—until she gave him one ultimatum too many.

The waiting moments dragged into an hour, then two hours. The conversations in the hospital corridors lapsed into hushed comments and whispered expressions of concern. Every door that opened and every person in surgical garb who rounded the corner heightened the shared anxiety.

PASTOR, WILL YOU PRAY?

Finally, a weary surgeon with a mask dangling from one ear walked slowly into the room. You could feel, almost hear, the hush of the moment.

"Ethel," he asked with a sigh, "where has Jake been living in recent weeks?"

"Well . . . ah . . . he's been living away from our house," she answered hesitantly with eyes lowered. "I don't know his address but I've been told it's in one of the lower income sections of the city. He has a new job and it's hard to make it on one income, especially when you pay rent on two places, and . . ."

"And where has he been eating?" the surgeon interrupted impatiently.

"I really don't know," she replied uncomfortably as she glanced at me. "I guess he's been eating at some of the diners and dives near where he's been living. Why do you ask?"

"Because, Ethel," the doctor answered in frustration, "I've just removed from Jake's intestines a mass—a mass . . . a mass of undigested . . ."

The surgeon took a deep breath and Ethel gasped.

"A mass" he repeated through clinched teeth, "of undigested *chicken dumplings!*" He then wheeled around and without another word, stalked out of the room.

Silence. Stunned silence.

"Pastor, will you lead us in prayer?" someone asked.

I muttered some kind of answer, asked everyone to bow his head, and for the first—and only—time in my life, thanked the Lord for *chicken dumplings*.

So, you're not feeling well today?

Cheer up—it could be chicken dumplings!

"AIN'T GONNA HAVE NO MORE!"

I parked my car alongside the curb, turned off the ignition, and sighed. There was something sad about the visit I was about to make. Dear old Mr. and Mrs. Darby, faithful members of our church through the years, were confined to their home. The aging process and the frailties of life had finally caught up with them. He was ninety-four years of age and she was ninety. Both had been in the hospital recently and neither was able to adequately care for the other. He had suffered a stroke, leaving his right side paralyzed, and she battled a cancer that sapped her energies. They were little more than shells of their former selves.

I got out of the car and glanced around as I made my way up the steps to the front door. Everything seemed to be aging right along with the couple who lived inside. The lawn, once manicured and immaculate, was brown and thirsty for water. The scattered patches of grass were dry and brittle. Only the weeds grew. The window boxes designed for colorful blooming flowers were filled with tired, withered stalks of what had once been. The old car in the driveway, idle and unused for weeks, was powdered all over with dust and grime. Two rocking chairs on the front porch had been turned backwards and leaned against the wall, a silent signal that late evening chats with friendly neighbors had finally come to an end. The paint around the door facing had peeled, and taped across the doorbell was a handwritten note that read, "Out of order." Somehow, that little sign, obviously written with a shaky hand, summarized everything.

It's not fair, I mused. *It's just not fair! It's not right for good people like these to come to the end of life with so many things "out of order."*

How on earth can I hope to say anything at all that might help this elderly couple?

But pastoral duty called, and for the moment I laid aside my own frustrations and knocked lightly on the door.

IT HAPPENS TO EVERYONE

"Mr. Darby . . . Mrs. Darby—it's Bruce, the pastor of your church."

I pressed my ear near the door and listened as a weak voice invited, "Come to the back door."

I walked around the house, climbed some rickety steps, and raised my hand to knock again.

"Come on in, Pastor; the door's not locked."

I hesitated, then stepped through the door, wondering again what in the world I could say or do to minister to their spiritual and emotional needs. This was unexplored territory for me. I was a young minister and these folks were walking slowly and painfully down paths that I had never traveled.

"Good to see you, Pastor," Mr. Darby said as he slowly waved a trembling hand at me from his recliner chair. "I'd get up to greet you but I'd probably fall, and you'd have to try to pick me up. And I don't think that's in your job description," he added with a chuckle.

I was relieved to hear the chuckle. So familiar. So encouraging. I had heard that chuckle of his in tedious committee meetings at the church, and had felt with others the immediate easing of tensions. I had heard it in the crowded hallways as I threaded my way toward the sanctuary for the worship service, wanting to be friendly to people but feeling the urgency of being on time. I had heard it—that special chuckle of friendship—at the close of a sermon when I knew better than anyone else that I had failed miserably in my attempts to get my point across. That chuckle and a pat on the shoulder helped pick me up and kept me going on more occasions than anyone could ever know.

Mrs. Darby, lying on a bed on the other side of the room, greeted me with a smile and a nod of the head. Her illness made speaking difficult, but the slight gestures and the kindness in her eyes expressed the warmth of friendship and welcome that I had felt so many times when I had visited with them. The world needed more people like the Darbys. For that matter, *I* needed more people like them.

"Yes sir," Mr. Darby continued, "it's so good to see you. Thank you for visiting an old, worn-out couple like us."

His greeting jarred me. It was hard, almost impossible, to think of this couple as "old," or "worn out." For a quarter of a century they had been involved in all aspects of the ministry of our church. They had unselfishly given their time, their money, and their prayerful support. The words "pillars of the church" had an authentic ring when applied to them.

"Now you just pull up a chair and have a seat," he continued. "Sorry we're not dressed for the occasion but the wife and I are being kinda lazy today. Hope you don't mind."

"Not at all, Mr. Darby. I just wanted to drop by and let you know we're all thinking of you and praying for you."

For the next few minutes we talked about the church, mutual concerns, and my family. They asked about each of the girls—Kathie, Shannon, and Renie—and wanted to know every little detail about their lives. I shared some of the latest "stories" from the McIver household and they responded with smiles and more chuckles.

This was not the time for a lengthy visit. I didn't want to tire them out and knew they both needed rest, so I suggested that it was time for me to leave.

"I'll be back in a few days," I promised as I stood. "Meanwhile, let's have a prayer together before I go."

"That'll be fine," Mr. Darby replied, "but first I want to talk to you about something."

A WISE CONCLUSION

"Of course," I answered as I sat back down. I wondered what was on the mind of this ninety-four-year-old man. Did he want to talk about his health? His will? The church? Some unfinished business? Death, or dying? Maybe plans for their memorial services?

"Pastor," he began seriously, "my wife and I had a discussion this morning."

"Yes, Mr. Darby," I responded in genuine concern. "Would you like to talk about it?"

"You know, Pastor, that we've had three children."

"Oh, yes," I replied. "I know them well."

"Now, since you know them well," he continued, "you also know that none of them turned out right."

Gulp.

How in the world was I to respond? My pastoral care class in the seminary didn't prepare me for this. The truth is I *did* know his children and, although I would never have dared say it, they really *didn't* turn out right. Thankfully, the old gentleman didn't wait for any reply from me.

"So, the wife and I talked it over this morning, and we came to a conclusion."

This time he did pause for my reaction.

"Yes? And what was your conclusion?" I asked.

He straightened up in his recliner, lifted a bony finger for emphasis, and declared with finality . . .

"WE AIN'T GONNA HAVE NO MORE!"

And then he looked across the room at his wife . . . and chuckled. She mustered a faint smile—tender and affirming.

I doubled over and fell out of my chair—right there in their den—pounded the floor with my fists, and guffawed! Then, in absolute ministerial disarray, I picked myself up from the floor, held my sides, and laughed my way out the door. I was so rattled, I had forgotten to pray! I laughed all the way to my car, and I admit that at that very funny moment in history, I wasn't worried that I hadn't prayed with this beloved couple, or even concerned that the whole afternoon had failed to go as planned. All I could think about was the neighbors—and hope they weren't watching.

3

And the Two Shall Be One. . . .

It was a wedding service never to be forgotten and, hopefully, never to be repeated. Once was enough.

I glanced at my watch and noted that it was seven-fifty in the evening—ten minutes before the organ fanfare would be followed by the traditional bridal processional. I knew that excited bridesmaids were adding final touches as they nervously checked their dresses in front of full-length mirrors, lightly sprayed their hair again . . . and again, and eagerly made last-minute searches for the flowers they would carry when they soon walked down the aisle.

I knew, also, that the groom and his attendants were secluded in another room, making fun of one another as they tried to don ill-fitting tuxedos and wondered which way to turn the cummerbunds. Having participated in hundreds of wedding services, I knew that it was time for the conversation among the fellows to become louder and more intense as the "countdown" to eight o'clock began. Often in the midst of this verbal melee, someone would yell, "Quiet! Everybody listen up!" This would be the cue for the groom to check again and be sure the best man had the license and the ring. And it was time for everyone to check his zipper for the tenth time!

All of this is predictable. It's all part of the ritual of any wedding service. It seldom changes.

THE FATHER OF THE BRIDE

On this occasion I made my rounds. I tapped lightly on Angelia's dressing room door, told her how beautiful she looked, and wished her "God's blessings." I then headed down the hall to speak with Timothy when one of the church staff called, "Pastor, there's an urgent call for you."

"I can't take a call now," I answered impatiently. "I have a wedding service to perform in five minutes."

"You'd better take this one, Pastor. It sounds urgent."

Timothy would have to wait for the moment. Something serious could have happened to one of the members of the church. An accident? A death?

Maybe something was wrong at home. Lawanna? The girls?

I picked up the receiver and heard someone ask, "Pastor McIver?"

"Yes."

"I'm a friend of Angelia's family, Pastor, and I thought you needed to know that Angelia's father is on his way to your church."

"But Angelia told me he had refused to attend the wedding," I replied quickly. "She said he's a very angry man with a lot of deep problems, but he won't let anyone help him. Apparently he's been out of touch with her and her family for several months. That's why her uncle is giving her away tonight."

"I know all that, Pastor, but he's headed that way now."

"That's fine, but I hope he gets here in the next five minutes or he'll be late."

"No, Pastor, you don't understand. He's drunk—very drunk. He's a big man and says he's going to "shoot up" the wedding.

He's mean, sir; and when he gets drunk he gets *real* mean. If I were you, I'd be very careful."

I thanked the caller for alerting me, glanced at my watch—two minutes to go—and trembled all over.

"Lord," I mumbled, "when I told you I would preach, I thought that's what you wanted me to do. Frankly, Lord, there's enough tension in performing a wedding ceremony without having to look over my shoulder to see who's going to shoot me!"

Time was running out. One minute to go.

I dashed down the hall (as fast as a man with a bad hip and a chronic limp can dash!), opened the door next to the organ loft, and whispered to the organist, "Not yet; keep playing!"

He looked at me in surprise, nodded that he understood, and then uttered under his breath, "When?"

"I don't know," I whispered back. "We've got a problem. Just keep playing."

"PASTOR, HE'S MY BROTHER!"

I ran out the door and raced around the building to the rear of the sanctuary, hoping to intercept the bride and her attendants before they began the procession down the aisle. I was in luck. The bride was a couple of minutes late and had not yet arrived. But her uncle who was to give her away was standing there, dressed in his evening clothes and smiling ear to ear. I motioned for him to meet me outside the door.

"Something wrong?" he asked, noticing the obvious concern on my face.

"We may have a problem," I replied. "I just received a call that Angelia's father is on the way to the church. He says he's going to 'shoot up' this wedding. Do you think he'll really cause trouble?"

"Is he drunk?"

"Yes, very drunk."

"Well, Pastor, he's my brother and I hate to say this, but if he's drunk, he will cause trouble. Big trouble."

"What do you think we ought to do?"

"Call the police and have him thrown in jail. He's tough, and he weighs over two hundred and fifty pounds. I think you need to call the police right now. By the way, tell them he'll probably be driving a two-tone red and white Buick."

"I'll do what I can," I promised weakly. "I'm on my way to make some calls, but don't tell Angelia. She's got enough on her mind without having to deal with this."

"I won't tell anyone," he agreed as he stepped back inside the building. "I'll not let on to Angelia or any of the family that he's on his way here. Just make sure the police get here in a hurry."

"Lord," I mumbled again, "did he say two hundred and fifty pounds? And he's drunk? Please, Lord, I've got a sanctuary half-full of happy well-wishers, and I've got Angelia and her bridesmaids ready to march down the aisle. . . . and I've got a groom who would pass out if he knew what's going on. . . . and I've got an organist who's probably sitting up there whispering to himself, "When?" And I've got to make these calls. . . . and . . ."

I turned quickly and headed toward the office area to make the calls. Fortunately, Lieutenant Wayland Fields of the Dallas Police Department was in his office. I got through to him immediately. He was a good friend and a faithful member of Wilshire. Just the sound of his voice made me feel better—for the moment.

"Look, Wayland," I exclaimed excitedly, "I've got some problems out here at the church." I told him briefly what had happened, described the father of the bride, and gave him information on the car he would be driving.

"You go ahead and begin the ceremony," he replied. "I'm dispatching three units immediately. They will be there in ten minutes. I'm also on the way myself. This will be a priority code, but we'll not have the lights and sirens on. I don't want what we do to add to the disruption."

I thanked him and breathed a prayer of gratitude for all policemen—especially those who protected ministers at weddings!

I then scurried out the office door and headed down the hall to whisper to the organist, "NOW."

Ten paces later I bumped into John Bowen, one of our church custodians. John was a delightful black friend about thirty years of age. He was tall, fine looking, well-built, and had salt-and-pepper hair that made his appearance even more distinctive. He had a warm spirit and a kind, soft voice. John was always ready to do anything anyone asked of him, and most of the time the asking was not necessary. He was a valuable member of the staff.

"John," I blurted out without thinking, "There's a big man . . . two hundred and fifty pounds . . . he's drunk . . . and he's on his way to the church right now. He says he's going to shoot up this wedding. Now, John," I continued without taking a breath, "I've just called the police. Lieutenant Fields is on his way and he's dispatching three other units."

John's eyes got bigger and bigger and his mouth fell open.

"John, I want you to go to the back of the sanctuary. Don't tell anybody you know what's happening, but for heaven's sake (and mine!), don't let any two hundred and fifty-pound man with a gun in his hand through that back door!"

John didn't say a word. He just looked at me, mouth wide open.

"I gotta go now, John. I'm telling the organist to begin the processional. Thanks for helping."

"LORD, PLEASE PROTECT US!"

Ten minutes later the bridal procession was finished and fourteen smiling attendants surrounded the nervous but happy couple. Angelia and Timothy had never looked more radiant. Somehow I managed to get through the introduction of the ceremony and through an opening prayer. How I prayed!

For blessings, and for guidance . . . and for protection. Especially for protection!

Then someone sang the "Lord's Prayer." While others bowed their heads and closed their eyes, I peeped. To my delight I discovered my prayer for protection had already been answered. Through the glass in the doors at the rear of the sanctuary I saw Lieutenant Fields. He was wearing his dress uniform and his braided white cap. He was standing tall and erect against the double doors with his arms folded across his chest in an authoritarian stance. He must have had a feeling that I was peeping for he nodded ever so slightly in my direction and smiled at me. I do believe he looked like an angel that night!

The rest of the ceremony went off without a hitch. The rings were exchanged and the vows spoken. I pronounced Angelia and Timothy "husband and wife"—to the joy of those in attendance. The recessional was celebrative. I exited through the side door—with hardly a limp.

The two hundred and fifty-pound father was apparently so drunk he never found the church.

Angelia and Timothy never knew about his threat.

Thirty years later, they still don't know.

The crowd had dispersed. The bride and groom had dashed to their car in a traditional shower of rice. The family and most of the wedding party had gathered up tuxedos and other garments and headed for home. The organist, with a sigh of relief, had closed the console. I made my way through the small kitchen adjacent to the reception hall, hoping for a cup of soothing coffee or a hot punch. The drama was over. I was grateful and ready to get on with life.

A LIKELY STORY

At that very moment, I spotted John, the custodian, sitting on the floor next to the stove with his legs drawn up and his chin on his knees, looking like he was in a helpless, semi-fetal position.

"Hi, John," I said.

Not a word. Not even a glance upward.

"Something wrong, John?"

Slowly, ever so slowly, he raised his head and looked at me with eyes as big as saucers.

"Pastor," he said, barely above a whisper, "don't you . . . don't you *ever* do that to me again."

It took a moment for his words to sink in.

"I'll do anything you ask," he said in measured tones, "except guard doors at weddings."

I laughed, and after a long moment, he managed a weak smile.

Still later that night, after I had gone home. . .

John and the other custodian, Denver, were turning out the lights and closing up the building. It was nearly midnight.

"John," Denver said, "I've been having trouble with my car lately. The batteries seem to be weak. Would you mind waiting on the parking lot until I see if it will start?"

"I'll be glad to."

Denver got in his car, put the key in the ignition, but nothing happened. Sure enough, the battery was dead.

"I've got some jump cables in my car," John offered. "Let me pull up next to you on the parking lot and see if we can get it running."

John walked across the lot, got into his own car, and drove it over next to Denver's. He raised the hood, connected the battery cables, and froze as he heard the squeal of tires as three Dallas police cars—with red lights flashing this time—screeched to a stop and surrounded them!

It took a lot of tall talking for John to convince the policemen that he was not the man they were looking for—even if his own car *was* painted two-tone red and white!

It wasn't long afterwards that John resigned as custodian and began selling insurance.

I figure he found it easier to deliver death benefits than to risk his life guarding doors at weddings.

4

"Grow Old Along with Me!"

Jean, my first wife and Kathie's mother, died at the young age of thirty. Polio. Our only child, Kathie, had just turned four, and I was unprepared—woefully unprepared to be a "single parent." By the way, this was long before they had discovered the term.

A few days after Jean's memorial service, it hit me: Kathie and I were on our own—alone—in our duplex in Dallas. It wasn't that family members didn't want to help. They did, but distance and health conditions and a variety of other situations made it inadvisable, if not impossible, for them to step in and assist on a day-by-day basis. Their moral support, prayers, and loving concern meant more than they could ever know.

A lot of things hit me without announcement in this "single parenting" role that had been so suddenly thrust upon me:

- sitting in the surgery waiting room with fourteen mothers while my child was having a tonsillectomy

- rearranging work schedules so I could attend PTA or "Bluebirds"
- looking the city over for a blue Christmas tree just because Kathie wanted a blue one, and trying to explain that to neighbors who have never had, or even seen, a blue Christmas tree
- standing outside a toilet in a public place, hoping some kind lady would understand and help retrieve my little girl who refused to come out
- explaining to Kathie that I couldn't marry that nice lady—because she was already married . . . to a deacon in my church.
- and dreading holidays, vacations, family gatherings, and even "family suppers" and "family fellowships" at the church.

But with God's help, I learned quickly that life is lived day-by-day and the "dailiness" of it, as Mother used to say, is overwhelming.

"Daily" meant fish sticks and beef potpies and, for a change, chicken potpies. "Daily" meant rolling hair, trimming hair, and finally cutting hair—real short. "Daily" involved selecting clothes for a little girl (with the help of some dear friends), buying clothes, and washing clothes. "Daily" meant walks to the park, reading stories, and saying prayers at night. "Daily" also involved a rollercoaster ride through all the five-year-old childhood diseases—every one of them, or so it seemed!

But most of all, after the pangs of grief subsided, and after friends began talking about other things, "daily" meant experiencing the loneliness of existing in a suspended frame of time, with no clear perspective of the future. There was neither the time nor energy to talk about next year, or a new house, or a new job, or even new furniture.

Everything was daily; everything was on hold; life was pregnant with "meanwhile."

Then as time passed, friends began to talk . . . and tease.

"What about her?" or, "I know a friend;" or, "I saw her looking at you;" or, (worst of all) "You know, of course, Kathie *does* need a mother. . . ."

So like a little schoolboy, you begin to think . . . and wonder . . . and wait.

And wait.

The dating game finally begins, and for the most part it's a downer. You're too old to play games and too proud to run the risk of rejection and too independent to rely on well-meaning but sometimes unreliable friends.

And too tired to stay out late . . . and too poor to afford fancy dinners and expensive musical productions.

So you date . . . and hope . . . and wait . . . and pray. You pray a lot. And Kathie prays, to your chagrin and frustration, "Lord, give me a little brother or a little sister."

And you think you want a miracle but, "Lord, I'm not sure even *You* can pull this one off!"

Things don't work out once . . . twice . . . more. . . .

And you're glad.

"Lord, if it's not in Your will for me to find the right one—not just a mother for Kathie, but someone I can love with all my heart—then I'll try to understand . . . and adapt . . . adjust . . . and become the best 'single parent' ever."

And then came Lawanna. A gift. A gift from God . . . with an Indian name meaning "By the still waters."

As I was soon to realize, there's nothing "still" about her, but strangely, she calmed my heart . . . my life . . . and my home . . . more than anyone could ever imagine.

And she took the toil out of all those "dailies" and gave me a future.

DAD'S VOTE OF CONFIDENCE

When I called Mother and Dad on January 2 and told them that I had met the *very* girl and would be marrying, Mother asked, "What's her name?"

"Lawanna," I answered.

"When are you getting married?"

"February 13th."

Then Dad spoke up, interrupting with, "Son, why on earth are you waiting so long?"

(Frankly, if I had known then what I know now, I don't think I would have waited the six weeks until February 13!)

"Son, I'm happy for you," Dad continued. "Now, tell me, what's she like?"

"I'm not sure, Dad; but she's not like anyone else I've ever known."

"Marry her, Son. Don't you let her get away. Marry her!"

Dad's been gone a long time, and I discover each day new answers to his question, "What's she like?"

- She's a free spirit . . . but she's anchored to the basics.
- She's a wife who cares . . . but doesn't coddle.
- She's a mother . . . who knows how to play with her children (and now grandchildren).
- She's independent . . . but she's a gracious part of the whole.
- She's creative . . . without being strange.
- She's a concerned Christian . . . without a pinched look.
- She's "Lawanna" . . . still waters . . . and rippling currents.

And Dad, wherever she is, things have a way of "happening."

LAWANNA'S GREAT BANK ROBBERY ADVENTURE

Lawanna was on one of her trips back home to Anniston, Alabama, to check on her elderly parents, Walter and Delba House, and to enjoy a good visit with them. Her sister, Susie, lived in the area and was in touch with them daily, but Lawanna would spend three or four weeks a year with her parents to lend her own support. These were usually "working" visits for Lawanna—taking inventory of the pantry, cooking and storing foods in the freezer, and assisting with practical needs.

A couple of days before she was scheduled to return to Dallas she ran some errands in the downtown area of Anniston. As usual, she had more to do than she had planned and, as usual, time ran out. Late in the afternoon, after the sun had gone down and after darkness had settled in, she called to tell her parents that she would be a few minutes later than she thought.

When she finally reached home about six o'clock she was met by a concerned eighty-five-year-old father who said anxiously,

"Sister, it's dark outside; I don't like for you to be out on the streets after dark."

Lawanna, who has traveled the world over—in daylight and dark—humored her father by reassuring him that she had been very careful.

"But you never know what can happen out there after dark," he countered. "You just can't be too careful these days."

"I understand, Daddy; and I appreciate the love and concern you've always had for me. But I don't want you to worry about me. I'm nearly sixty years old and . . ."

"But there's all kinds of mean things happening out there after dark."

"Okay, Daddy, I promise I'll be very careful," Lawanna smiled, realizing that even as a grandmother she would always be a "little girl" to her father.

The next day there was another errand to run. Walter had a small Certificate of Deposit that had matured. Happily, he had learned that a bank in the adjoining town of Oxford, just over the mountain, was paying 2 percent more interest than he had been receiving. So he cashed the CD in, got a cashier's check for the amount, and asked Lawanna to drive him and her mother to the new bank. They agreed to leave late in the morning, transact the business, and then have lunch together at Morrison's Cafeteria. Shortly after 11:00 A.M. they were on their way. As they approached the bank, Delba sat quietly in the backseat while Walter watched for the entrance to the parking lot.

"Turn the car right here—right here, Lawanna," he said.

"But, Daddy, are you sure? The sign says 'exit.'"

"I'm sure. I've been to this bank before."

"But the sign says . . ."

Oh, well, rather than prolong the discussion from the middle of the street, Lawanna made a turn into the parking lot of the bank, entering with the arrow pointing in the opposite direction.

AN OMEN . . . WASN'T IT?

That should have been an omen of what was to follow.

"Mother, we won't be long," Lawanna said as she parked the car in front of the door and got out. "Why don't you just sit here while Daddy and I do our business? We'll only be a few minutes and then we'll go to lunch."

"Sounds good to me," Delba replied. "Take your time. I'll be fine out here."

Lawanna and Walter opened the front door and walked into a nearly empty lobby—empty and silent. Strangely silent.

"Looks like everybody's gone to lunch," Lawanna commented as she surveyed the room. There was one bank officer at her desk, assisting a customer in filling out forms, and there was one teller behind the counter, apparently taking care of a young man. "Daddy, you wait here. I'm going over to the counter and ask the lady if there's a place where you can sit and be more comfortable while you wait."

Walter protested mildly, insisting he was fine and did not need to sit down. Lawanna smiled, ignored him, and began walking across the lobby. The young man at the window finished his business, placed his things in a black backpack, turned, and walked straight toward Lawanna on his way to the door. Their eyes met and he stared at her boldly for several seconds. Then he continued walking casually out the door.

Before Lawanna could reach the counter the terrified, ashen-faced teller screamed, "We've been robbed! We've been robbed!" She then dashed across the lobby, ran past Walter who was still holding his cashier's check and still waiting for a "comfortable seat," locked the door, and sounded the alarm.

Within minutes the building was teeming with bank officials, security officers, policemen from both Anniston and Oxford, and FBI agents. As the first came through the door Walter whispered nervously to Lawanna, "I didn't see a thing; and if they ask you any questions, you didn't see anything either."

"I think I've already seen more than I bargained for!" Lawanna replied, wondering how in the world one could be on an errand of mercy for elderly parents and end up in a real-life "Bonnie and Clyde" adventure.

The officers and agents methodically and professionally went about their business. They dusted furniture and doors for fingerprints, removed and reviewed film, frame-by-frame, from the video cameras, and secured the building.

Meanwhile, Delba sat in the car . . . on the parking lot . . . wondering why the doors to the bank had been locked . . . and why all those bank customers were lining up outside the building . . . and why Walter and Lawanna had apparently been locked inside.

"My mother has been waiting outside in the car," Lawanna said anxiously to one of the officers. "She's not in good health, so you'll either have to let me out or you'll have to bring her in here."

DELBA'S FIRST BANK JOB

Two officers graciously escorted Delba in, ushered her to a plush leather chair, and brought her a soft drink. Delba was pleased. It was her first bank robbery.

Later, Lawanna was questioned at length by one of the FBI agents. "Lady, just relax and tell us what you can," he said in a calm voice. "The terrified teller followed carefully the man's note of instructions but couldn't give us any concrete information. The robber was very professional. He kept his head down and the bill of his cap covered most of his face, so the bank video camera isn't much help. We need any information you can give us. It appears that you are our only witness. Did you get a good look at him?"

"We stared each other in the eyes for what seemed like half a minute, eyeball to eyeball," Lawanna replied, "and then he ambled past me to the door. He was Caucasian, about thirty years of age, medium build, approximately five feet, ten inches, and I remember vividly . . . brown eyes."

"Can you give us a description of the clothes he was wearing?"

"He had on a loose-fitting green shirt—the same color people wear who work in medical centers."

"Anything else?"

"Yes, he had a dark backpack over his shoulder and he had a full, neatly trimmed mustache. For some reason by the time he reached me he had taken his cap off, so I could see his dark brown hair pulled into a pony tail, about collar length."

"That helps," the agent responded as he took notes.

"Now Mrs. McIver, is there any other general impression that you had that might be helpful to us?"

"As a matter of fact, there is," Lawanna answered. "I hope you'll understand what I'm about to say, but to a 'little old lady in tennis shoes' nearly sixty years of age, he was—well, he was rather good-looking."

The agent forgot that he was an agent. He lost it professionally as he collapsed across the desk, doubling up with laughter.

While he was still laughing, beepers, "walkie-talkies," two-way radios, scanners and whatever else policemen and agents carry with them went off.

"Armed bank robbery in progress! Armed bank robbery in progress! Colonial bank . . . just off Quintard Avenue . . . . . behind Wal-mart!"

The officers and agents raced out the door, dashed across the Wal-mart parking lot, and were just in time to give chase to the robber. They nabbed him as he attempted to escape in his stolen vehicle.

Same robber.

"How can you know he's the same one?" Lawanna asked the agent later.

"Your description helped, Lady," he said with a grin. "And by the way, he *is* sorta nice looking."

Nice looking or not, he was an escapee from a prison in Florida. He had been convicted of armed robberies—ten in all—and was serving a sentence of life without parole, so he had nothing to lose! He was being investigated for six other bank robberies—and now he had been caught in two more in one hour! Obviously, he worked fast.

Later Lawanna, Delba, and Walter sat over a delayed afternoon "lunch" at the cafeteria, compliments of the bank. As they finished dessert, Lawanna looked out the window and watched the sun sink slowly behind the mountains.

"It's getting late, Daddy," she said with a somber look on her face. "We'd better be moving toward home. It'll soon be dark, and, as you reminded me yesterday, a lot of *mean things can happen out there* after dark."

Walter guffawed. Delba grinned. Lawanna kept a straight face, and the three headed for the car.

TEA AT THE ROCKWELLS

"Lawanna, I've just found the perfect book for you to review next year," exclaimed long-time friend and house guest, Grady Nutt. "I've just finished reading *My Adventures As An Illustrator,* by Norman Rockwell, and it is a *must* on your list. Then he handed Lawanna a well-worn paperback edition of the autobiography.

"Read it and see for yourself," he added with a grin. Lawanna took the book and thanked Grady with a bear hug.

Professional book reviewing is a disciplined, demanding responsibility. It involves reading or browsing dozens of books, selecting the right autobiography or biography, working hundreds of hours condensing the contents of the book to one hour, memorizing the manuscript, and "crawling into the skin" of the author and presenting the material in first-person style. Lawanna had recently been introduced into the field. Resurrecting her background skills in speech and drama, she had picked up her "rusty tools" (as she put it) and moved into the competitive arena.

She soon discovered there are hundreds of civic and book clubs in the southwestern part of the United States. And she learned the hard way that a good reviewer will often speak four or five times a week before these various clubs. Lawanna was good.

"Grady, you are a God-send!" she exclaimed as she took the book from her friend. "You've helped me more than you can know. The hardest part of reviewing is finding the right book. If you say this is a must for me, I'll read it immediately."

Within three days she had finished the first reading, closed the book, and said with a sigh of relief, "Grady was right. I've found my book for next year."

ROCKWELL'S BOOK A HIT

Rockwell's book was read again and again in the coming weeks. It was marked, condensed, outlined, and committed to memory—just in time for the review season which began in September and lasted until May.

"There's just one thing lacking," she said to me one morning. "I really need a hard-bound copy of the book to display during the presentation. I've checked book stores all over Dallas and not one can be found. In fact," she continued, "there's only one copy for all of the public libraries in the city."

And, after checking with rare book dealers from the east to the west coast, she concluded that Rockwell collectors were not about to turn loose their copies.

"Why not go to the source?" I suggested. "Why not contact Norman Rockwell himself, tell him what you're doing, and see if he can help you?"

That's all it took. She sat down immediately and penned a note to him in Stockbridge, Massachusetts. She congratulated the illustrator on his eighty-second birthday (she'd read about it in the papers), wished him continuing health, and explained her dilemma.

To my surprise (but not hers) a handwritten reply came within a week. It seems that Rockwell was impressed that anyone would want to review his book—so impressed that he had personally searched for a good copy. He had found one—a first edition copy no less—in Melvin's Bookmark, located over a drugstore in Great Barrington. But Melvin wanted ten dollars for the book.

"Would ten dollars be too much?" Rockwell wrote.

Ten Dollars! Lawanna was excited enough to pay one hundred!

For the next several months she reviewed *My Adventures As An Illustrator*, by Norman Rockwell. She reminded her audiences that the artist had painted 318 covers for the *Saturday Evening Post*, each seen by an average of four million people. His works had appeared in or on every major magazine published in this land. His advertisements had sold air travel, bicycle tires, cough medicine, encyclopedias, fountain pens, insurance services, toothpaste, and scores of other products. In addition, he had illustrated the lives of Benjamin Franklin, Tom Sawyer, Huckleberry Finn, and an uncommon soldier named Willie Gillis.

Lawanna underscored in her reviews that Rockwell was, and is, "Americana at its best." His paintings illustrated everyday happenings in average America—the awkwardness of youth, family vacations, homecomings, visits to the family doctor, the comforts of old age, pride in country and heritage, and reverence for life. His portrayal of America with such affection brought him the title, "an interpreter of his nation's life."

The review season was almost over. Rockwell's book had been a smashing hit with audiences. Lawanna was already scheduled for several more years to continue sharing the illustrator's delightful story.

A PERSONAL NOTE

Then one day I came across Lawanna in her study . . . in a reflective mood. I could almost see the wheels turning in her mind as she sat there.

"Do you think . . . would it be presumptuous . . . do I dare . . .?" she mused to no one in particular.

"Why not!" she exclaimed as she reached for a pen and stationery.

"I am securing one of your "triple-self-portrait" prints," she wrote, "to frame for my personal memorabilia wall in our home. It would mean so much to me to have one of your worn, discarded paintbrushes—large or small—with or without bristles. I'd love to also frame it under your portrait."

Brilliant psychology! I thought. *Poor old Norman doesn't know what he's up against.*

A week later another note came from Rockwell. And along with the note was a carefully wrapped *autographed* paintbrush—with traces of paint still clinging to its well-worn bristles! This precious gift became all the more meaningful when it was announced a few days later that the elderly artist had painted his last picture and had laid down his brushes. Within a few months he was dead.

A short time later Lawanna visited with her friend, Sandra Gill, a member of our church and a collector of Rockwell memorabilia. She proudly shared the letters and the gift of the paintbrush.

"Why don't we make our own pilgrimage to Stockbridge?" Sandra suggested. "It'll give us the chance to see where he lived, feel the family atmosphere of the community, and maybe meet some 'locals' who knew him."

"That's a great idea" Lawanna replied excitedly. "One of my dreams has been to walk down Main Street, made famous in his 1967 *Christmas at Stockbridge* painting. Besides," she added, "it will give me the opportunity to visit with Kathie." Ironically, our oldest daughter, Kathie, with a couple of college degrees tucked away, was working at the time in Stockbridge as a piano accompanist and counselor for the "Beaupre Performing Arts" summer camp for young people.

"I'll make the reservations," Sandra offered. "We'll stay at the historic old Red Lion Inn." The hotel, built in 1773, was once a stagecoach stop and a pre-Revolutionary War meeting place. Several of Rockwell's original paintings graced the inn. It never occurred to Lawanna and Sandra that getting reservations at the hotel might be difficult. They were already packing their bags!

A few weeks later they checked into (you guessed it) the Red Lion Inn. Their third-story room overlooked (you guessed it, again) the quaint home of Norman and Molly Rockwell. The New England clapboard house, originally built in 1783, was surrounded by trees and a thick hedgerow. Rockwell's simple red-barn studio was immediately behind the house.

Lawanna, Sandra, and Kathie spent a week walking around the town center, visiting with locals who had modeled for the illustrator, browsing the picturesque shops depicted in the *Post* covers, touring the Town Hall, paying grateful homage at Rockwell's grave in the Stockbridge cemetery, visiting the small Old Cornerhouse Museum, and drinking coffee on the front porch of the inn.

Late one morning over a second cup of coffee, Lawanna mused half aloud, "Do you think . . . would it be presumptuous . . . do I dare?"

"What are you talking about, Mother?" Kathie asked.

"Kathie, go inside to the front desk and get me some hotel stationery and a pen," Lawanna responded with an all-knowing smile in her eyes.

Ten minutes later the note to Molly Rockwell had been written and sealed.

"WITH GRATITUDE . . ."

In it she expressed gratitude for the illustrator's help in securing the first edition, hardcover copy of his book and for the priceless gift of the paintbrush. She shared briefly with Molly the warm response of people to her husband's story through the book reviews, reflecting their continuing appreciation for "America's favorite painter." She closed with a word about the pilgrimage that she and Sandra were making and wished Molly the best.

The note was finished, but the problem had just begun.

"Let's walk across the street and put this in her mailbox," Lawanna said to Sandra and Kathie.

Good idea. But when they crossed the street they discovered there was no mailbox. Lawanna then remembered from her book reviews that the Rockwells *had* no mailbox. Instead, Norman's practice each day had been to paint during the morning hours, break for lunch, rest for an hour, and then ride his bicycle down Main Street to the post office to collect the mail. The exercise was good for him; so were the informal chats with the locals along the way.

On the other side of the street Lawanna surveyed the situation. The only thing separating her from the screen door of the house was a clump of thick trees and a hedgerow.

"I think . . . I think I can make it around the trees," she pondered, "and maybe . . . under the hedge."

"Mother, you wouldn't!" Kathie exclaimed.

But she would—and she did. On hands and knees she crawled under the hedge, slithered around the trees, and slipped the note under the screen door, listening to the stifled giggles of Sandra and Kathie in the background. Only as she struggled through the hedge again on her return did she realize she had been at the *back* of the house, not the front!

But, in spite of the misdirection, it was worth the effort for later that afternoon a handwritten note addressed to her was delivered to the hotel desk. Molly Rockwell had invited the three to coffee the next morning!

After an exciting sleepless night, they found the proper gate and walked up to the *front* door with all the dignity and poise they could muster. A lovely, gracious, white-haired Molly opened the door, invited them in, and thoroughly thrilled Lawanna by inviting her to sit in Rockwell's own easy chair. Over coffee for the next hour she talked about "her Norman," his work schedule, their children, and the "simple things" of life that meant so much to him. When the visit was over she graciously posed for pictures with Lawanna and thanked them for coming.

As they circled the house and passed by the thick hedgerow, Sandra reckoned out loud, "Wouldn't Norman have enjoyed painting you on your hands and knees, crawling under that hedge?"

"Yep," Lawanna giggled, "rear end and all!"

From what the curator of the magnificent new Norman Rockwell Museum told her on a later pilgrimage to Stockbridge, Lawanna is probably the only person who has a signed paintbrush from the artist.

And as far as we know, she is the *only* person who ever crawled under his hedge to get to his back door!

POSTSCRIPT:

Thirty-five years after marrying Lawanna, I can pray with all honesty, "Thank You, Lord, that in life some things do *not* work out. But, Lord, thank You that some things *do*."

A famous line from one of Robert Browning's most elegant poems goes like this:

> Grow old along with me!
> The best is yet to be,

The last of life, for which the first was made.
Our times are in his hand.[1]

That's how it is—how it's always been with Lawanna. Dad, she's a gift from the Lord . . . worth waiting for.

---

[1] *Bartlett's Familiar Quotations*, ed., Emily Morison Beck (Boston, MA: Little Brown and Company), p. 544.

5

Just Bark off the Old Family Tree

My brother, affectionately called "Sip" by family and friends, died suddenly a few years ago. I immediately caught a plane and flew home to North Carolina to help my sister and others make plans for the memorial services. These plans, as most families learn sooner or later, included setting the time and place for the service, purchasing the casket and other equipment necessary, writing an appropriate "obit" for the weekly paper (double-checking to be sure no name was left out and all names were spelled correctly), and selecting flowers, music, and the preacher.

And setting the time for "visitation."

As we worked through the details step by step, I discovered all over again that the visitation hour (actually two hours) is most important and could not be avoided. It's usually scheduled at the mortuary, or funeral home, the night before the memorial service to provide an opportunity for people in the community to do what the word suggests—visit. Family members, near and distant cousins, neighbors, old classmates, business associates, and a few who are just plain curious gather to express their feelings and share their sympathies. It's as much a part of the memorial process as any message by any preacher. It's woven into the fabric of social cultures.

So we scheduled it and promptly at seven o'clock the guests began arriving to pay their respects to "Sip" and to share prayerful concerns for the family. The open casket in the "viewing room" was banked with flowers, some of them bearing personal notes. Friends and relatives came from the hills and valleys, from creek banks and wooded areas, from neighboring villages and crossroads, and from the two-block-long main street in my home town.

It was really quite impressive—and moving. Obviously I had experienced some of this in my thirty-year pastorate in a growing church in the metroplex of Dallas, but not on this scale.

I was back home and fatigued as I was, I was grateful for the simple outpouring of kindness and love.

By 7:30 P.M. the funeral chapel was crowded with scores of good people, each voicing his own feelings and recalling his own special memories. That was the problem.

It's difficult for more than a hundred people to voice concerns and swap stories without raising their voices. The noise and din increased minute-by-minute, decible-by-decible until it was almost impossible to carry on any kind of conversation. This had nothing to do with lack of respect; it was just a matter of verbal survival. Before long it grew into a modified kind of "Baptist-Irish wake"—without the hard stuff.

A CAPACITY CROWD TURNS OUT FOR "SIP"

By eight o'clock the place was packed to capacity and I felt absolutely exhausted. It had been less than six months since my second open-heart surgery and I was drained, both physically and emotionally. Depleted. In desperation I looked around the room for some means of escape, but everywhere I turned I bumped into more people.

I paused, tried to collect my wits, and remembered what I had been taught in my recent post-operative therapy: "Create your own space . . . take a deep breath . . . relax . . . close your eyes . . . breathe . . . slowly and deeply. Now, find the rhythm. Good. Inhale . . . exhale; inhale . . . exhale; inhale . . . ex . . ."

On my third "exhale," with eyes tightly closed and hoping no one was watching, I had a strange feeling that someone had invaded my space. I opened one eye ever so slowly to check things out, and, sure enough, there he was—standing immediately before me . . . grinning.

"Remember me?" he asked with a chuckle.

Frankly, I've never known how to answer that question, especially if I don't remember the person. I've never been brazen enough to respond with a "Why should I?" or "I don't have the faintest idea." Neither have I had the courage to do what my friend, Ross Coggins, did at a national convention. He printed in tiny letters on his lapel identification badge, "I can't remember *yours* either."

But in this case, in the middle of the viewing room, I really didn't have a clue, so I just stood there with a blank look on my face and a sinking feeling deep down inside as this stranger just kept grinning back at me.

His closely cropped thin hair accentuated his round, ruddy face. His tight-fitting, multicolored sports coat with wide lapels, vintage seventies, made him look even larger than he was. His narrow black tie, vintage sixties, was obviously worn only on "special occasions." And Sip's death certainly qualified as one of those.

"Oh, c'mon," he urged. "You remember me. *Sure you do!* Try hard."

LEROY WHO?

"Well . . . ah . . . golly . . . I'm trying," I stammered.

"Me and you used to play together down on the farm when we was little boys," he persisted.

I had no idea what farm, but I did some quick calculations and figured that "little boys" meant at least sixty years ago. And I had lived in Texas nearly fifty of those!

"I'm trying," I struggled, "I'm still trying."

"Sure you remember," he teased with kind eyes, "I lived a few miles down the road from you."

That information didn't help a bit.

"I'm sorry," I pleaded. "You'll have to forgive me. I've had a lot on my mind today, and it has been a long time since . . ."

"Shucks," he said as he jabbed me good-naturedly on the shoulder. "Don't worry none about it. Name's Leroy."

Leroy? I thought. *Leroy who? I know a dozen people named Leroy, but they're all in Texas.*

I struggled to play it cool, took another deep breath (just like the therapist had taught me), shook hands with him, and said as positively as possible, "Oh, Leroy, so good to see you. Thank you for coming."

He didn't let go of my hand. Instead, he held on, looked me straight in the eyes, and studied me carefully.

"Yep," he added, "you and me and Sip all three used to play together on the farm. Always did like you brothers."

His voice trailed off then as he looked over at the open casket six feet from where we stood.

"You and Sip," he mumbled half to himself. "Bruce and Sip. Sip and Bruce."

By now it was obvious that Leroy was confused. He released my hand, took a step backwards, and sized me up again. He put his hand on his chin and turned a second time toward the casket in perplexed silence.

WHO'S WHO?

Then after what seemed like half an eternity, he took a deep breath, turned back to me and asked quizzically, "Let's see, are you him? Or is that *you* over there in the casket?"

I strangled, swallowed hard, stifled my feelings, and motioned to Lawanna who was standing in the middle of the crowd a few feet away. I turned my head away from Leroy and mouthed the unspoken words, "Get me out of here—NOW!"

Poor Lawanna read my lips and panicked. She thought my heart was acting up (it was!), pushed around people, grabbed my arm, and escorted—or dragged—me out of the room.

"Helen," she called, "open your office door immediately! Something's happened to Bruce!"

Helen Buckner, a favorite cousin, was the owner of the funeral home. She quickly opened the door, grabbed me by one arm while Lawanna held the other, and ushered me to her own office chair behind the desk.

"Quick!" Lawanna blurted. "Call a doctor."

"Don't bother," I strangled hysterically as I collapsed across the desk. I'm OK. At least, I think I am."

"But please close the door," I pleaded, "and keep everybody out—especially a guy named 'Leroy.'"

I then told them what had happened.

"One other thing," I added, wiping tears of laughter from my eyes, "Go out there and take another look at Sip. *Then let me know if I'm him, or if he's me!*"

Postscript: "visitations" are a part of life—and death. I wouldn't try to change that. Leroy meant well. I survived. And I know Sip would have loved this story.

TRAVELING . . . TOGETHER?

Speaking of my brother, "Sip". . .

For many years he owned a monument company in North Carolina.

It was a "full-service" kind of operation. A customer could choose a marble or granite stone from the display lot, order it cut to the proper size, select designs and inscriptions to be engraved on the stone and determine the date when it would be placed, or "set," in the cemetery. It was a good business for my brother, but it was also a helpful ministry to families.

On one of my infrequent trips back home I enjoyed browsing through the display lots, reading the inscriptions engraved on purchased headstones. They varied from marker to marker, often reflecting more sentiment than theology: "Asleep," "Angel," "Now Singing in the Angelic Choir," "Waiting for the Sunrise," and "Peace," or "At Rest."

One day I stumbled across a huge double headstone that grabbed my attention. It was cut out of some of the most beautiful granite to be found anywhere, and neatly engraved across the center in large letters was the family name. Then, on the left side of the marker was the name of a man and the dates of his birth and death. A casual glance told me that he had recently died. That same glance told me that somebody had spent a lot of money—big bucks—on the marker.

What intrigued me most, however, was the carving just above the family name. It was not an angel or a harp or a sunset. It was a perfectly proportioned engraving of a Winnebago motor coach. Just beneath the Winnebago were the words, "Traveling Together Through Life."

I turned in bewilderment and asked Sip, "What in the world does this mean? There's bound to be a story here somewhere."

"Well, there is," he replied. "This couple lived in a town not too far from here, and when they retired they bought this motor home. It was a dream come true for them and for two years they traveled happily across the nation together in their new 'home.' She said they had some of the best times ever on these trips. Then the man became ill and died suddenly. The grieving widow came in a few days later and picked out this stone—one of the nicest on the lot. When the purchase was completed she made an unusual request. She asked if we could engrave a replica of their motor home on the stone. And," Sip continued, "she said she wanted 'Traveling Together Through Life' under the engraving."

ETCHED IN STONE

Sip told me that he had secured a picture of the motor home and he and his crew made the appropriate line drawings on the stone. The sandblasting began and within hours the family name, picture, and words were permanently etched—a testament to family devotion, enjoyment, and togetherness.

It was a sweet story. I was almost moved to tears—and I didn't even know the people.

A year later I was back home, once again browsing through the monuments on display. I came upon one and did a double-take.

"Hey, Sip," I called. "Here's this Winnebago. You engraved this stone a year ago. Why is it still here on your lot instead of in the cemetery? What happened?"

"I really don't know the whole story," he replied. "But the widow came by and paid me what she owed. She told me that she had married another man, canceled the order, and then she and her new husband took off in the Winnebago, waving and smiling as they drove away."

The last time I visited the monument display lot, a few months before Sip died, I checked and the "Traveling Together Through Life" stone was still there.

But there was no sign of the Winnebago.

GRAMPA MOODY AND THE MAYO BOYS

I dialed my mother's telephone number and waited nervously for her to answer. The variety of strange tones—bleeps, hums, buzzes, and muffled bells—reassured me that the communication system was straining to make the journey all the way from Texas to North Carolina. I was grateful. And I was also grateful that new technology had replaced "operators" who had usually asked, "City, please?"

"Siler City," I would reply proudly.

"How do you spell it?"

"S-i-l-e-r C-i-t-y," I spelled slowly with mild irritation. I couldn't imagine that anyone didn't know where my hometown was. Even Andy Griffith talked about it frequently on his television series. Why, there isn't a "Mayberry" in the whole state of

North Carolina, but there's certainly a Siler City, and everybody ought to know how to spell it. Or so I thought.

"And what is that town close to?"

"Greensboro," I would answer with growing impatience.

After a lengthy pause, while I wondered if the telephone company's meter was ticking and if I would be charged for all this research, the operator would finally say, "Thank you. I've found it."

And then the inevitable question: "Now, what is the number you wish to call in Siler City?"

"Eight-F" I would respond meekly.

"Yes?" Hesitation. "And the other numbers?"

"Eight-F! There aren't any more numbers. Just plain 8-F!"

"Oh, I see. Just a minute, sir." Another pause.

Finally, "Here it is. Stand by and I'll ring. That's two shorts and a long."

The whole process was downright humiliating. I was proud of my hometown, my roots, and my friends. But "8-F" for a telephone number? Two shorts and a long? Frankly, I was grateful for a new day when weird digital sounds replaced the southern drawls of inquiring operators.

My recollections, punctuated with a hint of a smile, were interrupted by Mother's voice:

"HELLO—HELLO. ANYBODY THERE? HELLO."

Mother, like most of her brothers and sisters, had experienced hearing difficulties in the aging process of life. Just trying to communicate by telephone was a difficult, draining experience—for both of us.

"Mother," I spoke loudly into the mouthpiece, "I've got some great news. It looks like my hip can be fixed."

"Your WHAT can be fixed?"

GOOD NEWS FOR AN OLD MALADY

"My HIP, Mother. There's a new procedure that's been developed—a new operation—and the doctors out here seem to think that it might work in my case."

I was thrilled to be able to share the news with her. For forty-one years I had limped through life with a medically fused hip. My problems had begun with osteomyelitis, a bone disease that settled in the hip joint when I was a boy of nine—several years before the availability of penicillin and other "miracle drugs." Three major surgeries, months of hospitalization, numerous blood transfusions, daily doses of horrible-tasting cod liver oil, and a body cast that eliminated all motion in the hip until the joint became solid bone got me through the worst of the crisis—and through the next four decades.

Now there was hope that the long-term fusion could be reversed. A new hip joint seemed possible. Obviously it was too late for me to participate in sports activities, but just the thought of bending, twisting, and stooping like other people elated me. I wanted to share this with Mother, but I didn't want to cause her any worry about another operation. We'd been through enough of those.

"Mother," I continued, "my doctors in Dallas think the surgery can be done, but they want me to go to the Mayo Clinic for further evaluation."

"That's wonderful, Son," she replied. "The Mayo Clinic is a fine place to go for help. I know all about it."

I was confused by her answer. I knew that Mother knew about the Chatham Hospital, a small hospital located in our hometown; and, of course, she knew about Duke Medical Center where I had been a patient as a boy; and there was the Matheson Clinic fifteen miles down the road at Pittsboro. But the Mayo Clinic?

"No, Mother," I replied firmly, but politely, "I'm talking about another clinic. It's one of the best in the world; it's located in Rochester, Minnesota. It's a diagnostic clinic that specializes in unusual and difficult cases."

MOTHER KNEW ALL ABOUT THOSE MAYO BOYS

"I know all about that clinic," she interrupted with uncharacteristic impatience. "I know what they do there, and I know all about the Mayo brothers, Charles and Will. Those boys operated on Pa."

I couldn't believe what I had just heard. Mother—bless her heart—must have had difficulty hearing me, or understanding me. *After all*, I reasoned, *it's a long way from Rochester to the rural area of North Carolina. And the Mayo brothers operating on my Grandpa, Jasper Moody? No way*. I smiled to myself and ended the conversation by telling Mother that I loved her and that I hoped to visit with her soon. Meanwhile, I filed "Grandpa's surgery" and the Mayo brothers in the back of my mind.

But it wasn't in the back of Mother's mind. It was the first thing she wanted to talk about on my next visit home. The truth is, I think she was a little vexed with me because I questioned her in our telephone conversation. She insisted that I pull up a chair and listen. Like an obedient child I did, and I heard the full story for the first time.

The year was 1914. Mother, then an older teenager, was staying temporarily at home with her parents between teaching responsibilities in neighboring communities. "Ma" and "Pa," as she called them, lived on a farm in Chatham County. They were poor but they had been able to grub out enough from the raw land to feed and clothe ten children and see most of them move on to other places and other responsibilities. Their farmhouse was a mile from the Rives Chapel Church, located on Tick Creek—five miles from Bonlee, six miles from Ore Hill, and seven miles out in the country from Siler City.

But most of these towns and crossroads might as well have been a hundred miles away, for hard work and poor roads made travel anywhere difficult. So like most everyone else, they lived of necessity in their own world—struggling with the soil, harvesting the meager crops, helping neighbors who were in trouble, gathering at the church house on Sundays, and sharing stories and laughter after an evening's meal. Telling stories—and embellishing them—was at times the only entertainment they could afford. And they were good at it.

One day, according to Mother, Pa had the stomach ache. Ma put him to bed and treated him with all the home remedies available. Throughout the day and into the next his condition worsened. Finally, one of the boys got on a horse and rode to Ore

Hill to get Dr. Stroud, an old country doctor who for years had been the only physician in the area. The kind man listened to the need, hitched his best horse to a buggy, picked up his medical satchel, and two hours later arrived at the Moody farmhouse.

"He examined Pa for several minutes," Mother said, "while all of us children stood on the porch wondering what he would say. We knew that Pa was a mighty sick man."

"Then," she said, "Dr. Stroud left the room, walked past us, and motioned for Lee to come with him." Lee was one of the older boys in the family.

A FASCINATING DRAMA

"The two of them walked slowly down to the corn crib and spoke in hushed tones. I can still see them down behind that crib," Mother added with a faraway look in her eyes, "talking seriously and quietly to each other. I kept watching them and wondering what they were saying. I had a feeling it was bad. Finally, they headed back toward the house and when they reached the old well, Ma and the rest of us met them.

"We listened without saying a word as the doctor spoke. 'Mrs. Moody,' he said softly, 'your husband is a very sick man. He seems to have a growth either in his stomach or intestines. It's so big I can feel it. But I'm afraid I can't help him. There just doesn't seem to be anything that can be done. It's a matter of time. I'm so sorry.' Then, with a long look on his face, he climbed into his buggy and drove off."

By now Mother was re-living the story, re-creating the experience as she told me the story. The tale had come to life. I listened in rapt fascination. I was a child again . . . at my mother's feet.

"We all stood around the well in disbelief," Mother continued. "We were stunned . . . overwhelmed . . . too shocked to cry."

"Then one of the boys said, 'We're not just gonna stand around and do nothing and let Pa die. Not 'til we've done everything we can. I heard there's a new doctor in Siler City—a Dr. Wren. Let's go get him. He might see something different.'"

Courage. Dogged determination. Those were trademarks of the family, and they started with Pa and rubbed off on the children. Jasper Moody had seen his own father stumble home from the Civil War, crippled for the rest of his life; he had lost two brothers and a sister—all three at the same time—with typhoid fever; he and Ma Moody had built their first farmhouse, only to see it go up in smoke and flames a few hours after he made the final payment on the money borrowed to build the house; and he had watched crops devastated by droughts and by rains.

Through it all he had been a survivor. Now the family decided that it was time to try to keep on surviving.

So another horse was saddled, and one of the boys galloped off to Siler City to try to locate Dr. Wren. Several hours later the young doctor arrived and, once again, the children gathered around the old well in the yard while Pa was examined again.

"He's a very sick man, Mrs. Moody," the doctor said when he closed the door and walked out of the house. "There's not much hope for his recovery . . . unless we can get him to Greensboro and to the hospital there."

TO GREENSBORO, ABOARD THE "SHOO-FLY"

Greensboro? Why, Greensboro was nearly forty miles away, and Pa was dying. "But," my mother continued with a smile, "we didn't give up. I helped put a feather bed in the back of a wagon, the boys hitched up two horses, and several of us lifted Pa into the wagon. My older brother, Lee, and Dr. Wren then climbed up on the wagon and they headed for Ore Hill to catch the 'Shoo-fly.'"

"Shoo-fly?" I interrupted.

"Yes, the 'Shoo-fly.'" Mother said. "The 'Shoo-fly' was a little train that made a daily round trip between Greensboro and Sanford." I listened, and quickly calculated that the round trip distance would be about 150 miles.

"They knew that the train would be passing through Ore Hill late in the afternoon on its return trip to Greensboro, and they were determined to try to catch it," Mother added.

"When the train arrived they lifted "Pa" off the wagon and laid him down on the feather bed in the aisle of the train."

She paused and observed with gratitude, "That young doctor went with Lee and Pa all the way to Greensboro."

"What about Grandma?" I asked. "Didn't she make the trip?"

"Why, Son, there was no way Ma could go. Somebody had to run the farm and look after the children."

I continued to listen in silence, trying to comprehend the emotional impact of all this on a family as Mother kept talking. "The train pulled into the station at Greensboro and they unloaded Pa. Somehow—I really don't know how—they got him to St. Leo's Hospital. The doctors immediately examined him and confirmed what Dr. Stroud and Dr. Wren had said. Pa did have a growth, and they said that exploratory surgery needed to be performed without delay."

I was hanging onto every word as Mother spoke. I felt that I had been riding on that wagon, chugging along on the "Shoo-Fly," and standing in the corridor of the hospital with my Uncle Lee and Dr. Wren while waiting for a verdict from the examining physicians.

THE BIG-CITY OPERATION

Mother took a deep breath and then continued the story. "The doctors in the hospital said the operation would be critical, but then one of them added, 'In a way, we are very fortunate. We have two outstanding young physicians visiting with us and they are teaching new techniques in surgery. They're from out west . . . Minnesota, I believe. They're brothers—Will and Charlie Mayo.'"

"Well," she said with a lilt in her voice, "before that day was over those two boys had operated on Pa. Just as everyone expected, they found a tumor the size of a grapefruit. They bypassed the tumor, sewed Pa up, waited two weeks, and then performed a second operation and removed it."

I sat at Mother's feet in stunned silence. Disbelief.

Mother then leaned her head back, closed her eyes, and pondered for a moment.

"Now, let's see," she said, "That was 1914. Pa died in '34. That means he lived another twenty years."

A VOTE OF CONFIDENCE

Slowly, trying to comprehend what I had just heard, I looked up into my Mother's face. It was a face of courage and strength. For a brief moment, I saw that family conference by an old well, a galloping horse, a bumping wagon and a feather bed, and a train called the "Shoo-fly." And, I think I heard someone out of the past say, "We're not just gonna stand around and do nothing. . . ."

"Son," Mother said quietly with a knowing smile, "You make your plans to go to the Mayo Clinic. There's some mighty good people there."

And I believed her.

Then her voice trailed off as she added again, "Those boys operated on your Grandpa."

6

"But It Hurts Too Much to Laugh!"

I leaned back in my recliner chair, gently nursed a now-tepid cup of coffee, and stared blankly through the window into the pre-dawn darkness. The rest of the family was still asleep but the agonizing hours of tossing and turning were over for me. "Lord, be patient with me," I mumbled half aloud, "I'm trying to understand, but things just don't make sense."

In the middle of my pitiful (and self-pitying) whimper the telephone rang. *That figures*, I reasoned with half a smile, for I had learned as a pastor that Alexander Graham Bell's "gadget" had no respect for persons or privacy. It had the unique ability of intruding at the most inopportune moments—day or night. Or at six-thirty in the morning. I wasn't sure what heaven would be like, but I was confident of one thing: there would be no telephones. A compassionate God would simply not allow them there!

"Hi, Bruce," a bouncy, cheerful voice greeted me, "this is Bill."

The introduction was not necessary for I recognized the voice immediately. Bill O'Brien, a close friend, once served as Minister of Music at Wilshire. While on our church staff he and his wife, Dellanna, made commitments to serve as missionaries in Indonesia. And while on our staff he introduced me to Lawanna and later sang at our wedding. So the ties with Bill were deep and personal. I was glad he and his family were home on furlough after a four-year tour of service abroad. I was also glad they were living nearby in Fort Worth and we had opportunities to visit with them.

But I was not glad that he called this morning. I just wasn't in the mood to talk to anyone, not even a friend.

"How are you, Bill?" I asked, forcing the question.

"Oh, I'm great," he replied. "And you?"

There was an awkward silence, a silence that probed hidden thoughts and invaded realms reserved only for trusted friends.

"You haven't heard what's happening in my life?" I asked hesitantly.

"I don't know a thing."

"Then why did you call?" I asked innocently.

"I don't know," he replied, "I really don't know."

Bill didn't know. Few people did. Lawanna and I were still in shock and trying to absorb the jolting diagnosis. We were busy asking our own questions, nursing our own wounds, and wondering about the future. There just wasn't enough energy left to call others and try to fill them in.

So in that early morning hour, over cold coffee, I verbalized for the first time what had happened. I shared with Bill results of recent heart stress tests, follow-up visits with my internist and cardiologist, an overnight hospitalization for further tests, and the verdict of all involved: heart surgery immediately.

I also told Bill that I had resisted every test and denied every result recorded. I found some release of tension as we laughed together over my stubbornness and my "mule-headedness." And in a more subdued tone, I shared the news that the surgery would be scheduled immediately.

AN ENCOURAGING WORD

"Then this is why I called," Bill stated positively. "Listen carefully," he continued, "I got up early this morning to read my Bible before a seven o'clock graduate class I'm taking in the seminary. I read the sixth chapter of Judges, and for some reason I was impressed to write your name beside three verses—12, 14, and 16." I want you to get a copy of *The Living Bible*," Bill added hurriedly, "and read for yourself those verses. Sorry, but I gotta run. Nearly late for that class. I'll talk with you later today."

I hung up the phone, poured out the cold coffee, replenished it with a fresh cup, and mused over the conversation with my friend. *Strange conversation*, I thought. *Not like Bill at all . . . too early in the morning . . . devotional Bible reading in Judges (of all places!) . . . handing out verses of scripture to a person steeped in the mire of life . . . No, not like Bill at all.*

But out of curiosity I found The *Living Bible* and checked the verses.

". . . Mighty soldier, the Lord is with you" (v. 12).

". . . I will make you strong. . ." (v. 14) *Lord, I sure could use some strength!*

". . . But I, Jehovah, will be with you!" (v. 16).

I laid the Bible aside and slowly sipped the coffee. Nothing registered, except that I surely didn't feel like a "mighty soldier;" neither did I feel strong.

The sun came up. So did the rest of the family. The girls left for school and Lawanna made telephone calls to family members and friends, bringing them up to date on the test results and the anticipated surgery. Meanwhile, I sat and pondered. Life for me was on "hold."

About four o'clock in the afternoon, after a restless day, I paced through the den and saw a copy of a *New English Bible* on the end table next to the sofa. It had been a gift from Lawanna on Father's Day. I enjoyed the translation and used it occasionally in Bible studies and worship services at the church. It had a brown leather cover, excellent print, and a gold ribbon to mark special places. I casually picked up the Book and gently lifted the index ribbon and watched the Book open to . . .

Judges, chapter six.

Slowly, ever so slowly, I remembered.

The previous Wednesday evening, just before the heart test at the hospital, I had prepared to speak briefly at a prayer service at Wilshire. I had planned to talk about Gideon, a farmer and an ordinary man who was challenged to be a leader for God's people. But a children's choir had sung in that service and some special recognitions had been made. Time had run out. Before the benediction I had held up my Bible—this same brown Bible with the gold ribbon—and said with a smile to the people, " I came with a prepared message, but the time is up. The message can wait."

As I quietly stood in the den that afternoon and looked at the Gideon passage, I couldn't help but notice that verses 12, 14, and 16 had been clearly underlined for emphasis—the same three verses that Bill O'Brien had put my name beside.

Looking back . . .

The Lord must have said, "Bill, I've got a special job for you. Bruce prepared a Bible study last week and I tried to guide him in it . . . even impressed him to underline some verses that would have special meaning to him. But he's caught up in a lot of trauma today, and he's having a hard time remembering or believing anything. I need you to help me remind him. . . ."

Far-fetched?

I think not.

And I remember.

PAINFUL IN MILWAUKEE

"Mr. McIver. Mr. McIver!"

Somewhere in the distance a voice called, "Time to wake up."

I moaned, opened one eye in groggy confusion, and struggled to see. Where was I? What was going on? Who was calling? And was my name really "McIver?" After twelve hours of heart surgery, three full days—and nights—in Intensive Care, five days in a private room with endless comings and goings of medical teams and personnel, my body and I had finally collapsed in exhaustion. My last conscious thought had been, "Lord, please—just ten minutes of uninterrupted sleep . . . and I'll never ask for anything else!"

Gratefully, my prayer was answered, but I was given only *eight* minutes, not ten.

"Mr. McIver," a woman's voice called again, "time to wake up. We've got a lot of work to do this afternoon."

Work? My thoughts raced because I was too weak to talk. *She's got be to kidding. What kind of work?* My chest had been cut open and wired back together, my legs were throbbing from my heels to my thighs because of "scavenger searches" for veins healthy enough to be used in artery by-passes, my arms ached from IV tubes, and my throat was so dry that I could hardly swallow. Now, some ghostly voice had awakened me from the only sleep that I had had in days to tell me that we had "work" to do! And another thing—what was this "we" stuff? I was the only person whose name was on the door, and to my knowledge I was the only patient in the room.

My brain felt well enough to complain.

"Just a minute; I'll help you sit up." Then I heard the whir of the electric motor and felt the head of the bed begin to rise slowly. I blinked hard to focus my eyes on a figure in a white uniform, now standing next to me, who reached out and gently lifted me to a half-sitting position. For the first time I realized it was Nancy, my nurse from the day shift. She was my favorite of all the nurses—until that moment.

"Nancy," I mumbled. "You startled me . . . couldn't figure out what was happening . . . didn't know where I was. . . ." My words were slurred.

WHAT'S ALL THIS "WE" STUFF?

"You're fine, Mr. McIver," she said in a soft, reassuring tone. "You're in St. Mary's Hospital in Milwaukee, and you're doing great. Just a little sleepy right now, but you'll be good and awake before long. And then we'll get to work.

I didn't have the foggiest idea what she meant by "work."

"Here," she said as she handed me faded blue hospital pajama bottoms—the "one-size-fits-all" kind. Then she added, "I want you to put these on."

This was a new experience. For ten days I had worn a typical surgical gown that was designed to tie in the back. But since no one ever bothered to tie it, and since I couldn't reach around to tie the ends of the worn strings myself, the gown usually fell loosely over the front of my body. I had learned quickly how modesty was the last thing patients cared about following surgery.

"Please put the pajama bottoms on now," Nancy said as she moved toward the door. "I have to check on another patient but I'll be back in a minute."

I sat alone in the room. It was the first moment of privacy I had experienced in more than a week. Then, slowly and painfully, I reached down to try to put one foot, and then the other, into the appropriate leg holes of the pajama bottoms. Panting for breath and wobbling to keep my balance, I tugged and tried to pull them up. When they were just above my knees I stopped to catch my breath and looked down. I forgot all about Nancy, and our "work;" I even forgot about the soreness of my body as I slumped backwards on the side of the bed. Weak with fatigue, I gasped for strength and energy . . . . and then . . . something happened.

I laughed.

It hurt, but it was worth it. A ridiculous thought flashed through my mind. It came from a childhood memory back in my home state of North Carolina.

I remembered the changing colors of the leaves on trees in the fall, cold days and heavier clothing, long underwear and shoes that rubbed blisters on the heels. . . . and hog-killing time. . . .

Every November our family and most of the families around us went through the same ritual. The hogs that had been "slopped" and fattened for months were killed for bacon and ham and fatback.

And just as surely as November came, so did Johnnie Alston—a large, rotund, gregarious black man. I didn't understand it then, but Johnnie was essential to hog-killing season. Like the first frost and the falling of the first leaves, Johnnie arrived right on schedule. The old *Farmer's Almanac* was every family's guide and could have included under the prediction, "first freeze," the words, "Johnnie arrives." No one ever told me he was coming; I just knew.

HOG KILLING SEASON

Johnnie Alston would steer his 1931 Model A Ford pickup into the dirt driveway to our house, and chug across the backyard and through the open gate (we knew he would come), and into the small pasture where we kept our one milk cow. Johnnie would park his truck at the pigpen next to the small barn. The already limp, dead hog that had just been shot by my father would be loaded into the back of the truck and Johnnie would drive off and disappear.

It never occurred to me as a boy to ask where he was going, or why. Four or five hours later he would return in the same pickup with the lifeless hog bouncing in the back of the truck when Johnnie hit a bump—minus all hair and bristles. And minus also a few other parts that Johnnie got as payment for scrubbing and cleaning the hog. No one at our house ever complained about his price.

Johnnie fascinated me. I marveled that this loyal man could take a muddy pig that I had fed twice a day for months, load it in the back of his truck, drive away for a few hours, and then return it clean, slick, and almost white—ready to be carved up into hams and shoulders and tenderloins. Because of Johnnie, hog-killing was not work; it was an event.

Back in the hospital room, sitting on the side of the bed, I looked down at my own clean, white body that had been carefully washed and scrubbed and (heaven forbid!) thoroughly shaved for surgery a few days earlier. I smiled at the sight and chuckled softly. "Johnnie would be proud. And he would be especially proud of whoever 'prepped' me for surgery."

Thoughts of cold weather, falling leaves, and hog-killing times were interrupted when Nancy re-entered the room.

"Mr. McIver," she said in mild reprimand, "you haven't even tied your pajama bottoms. What have you been doing while I've been gone?"

"I'd tell you, but I doubt you'd understand," I whispered.

She wasn't curious because she was in a hurry. "Get those bottoms tied so we can get out of bed. We have a lot to do and we're already behind schedule."

Nancy's back into that "we" stuff, I thought.

Suddenly, the door burst open and Tonya, a hefty, no-nonsense hospital aide, marched in as if she owned the place.

Oh, no, not Tonya! I thought, but dared not say it out loud. Everyone, including the medical staff gave this woman plenty of room. She enforced rules and regulations, drove out visitors, made patients sit up and cough, adjusted and re-adjusted IVs, and pretended not to hear when patients cried out for mercy. Tonya "took no prisoners" on her wing of the hospital.

"All right!" she barked, "Everybody up. We're going for a walk."

I didn't have the strength or the courage to argue. I knew "everybody" meant me. I did believe, however, that someone should try to inject some sanity into this situation. So barely above a whimper, I muttered, "I'm not sure I can take a walk. Both legs are hurting badly this morning, and the sternum and ribs are sore, and . . ."

"Just move it, Buster," Tonya raised her voice. I trembled, and suspected that she was well experienced in situations like this. Golly, maybe she really *did* own the hospital!

"Yes Ma'am," I replied politely. Here I was, sixty-two years of age and just about as intimidated as I had ever been in my life. I felt like a little boy answering to his mother. Tonya meant business; so did Nancy.

PLENTY OF GOOD EXCUSES

"But I still have oxygen tubes in my nose," I pointed out hesitantly, "and the tubes are connected to a valve in the wall behind my bed. I can't leave the room without oxygen. Besides," I added hopefully, "I still have a large IV in my left arm."

"No trouble at all," Toyna clipped as she dragged a hideously green oxygen tank across the room and over to the side of my bed. She quickly switched the connections in one smooth, efficient motion. She then hurried to the other side of the room, grabbed a tall, skinny metal contraption, and wheeled it to the left side of my bed. Again, with precision she lifted the bag of intravenous fluid from the ceiling hook over my bed and hung it over the portable stand. She stepped back, surveyed the situation, and declared, "Now, on your feet; we're going to physical therapy."

Could this be real? Physical therapy? Was this really happening? I was too weary and weak to battle with words any longer. So I climbed awkwardly out of bed, stood shakily on my feet while Nancy took me by one arm, and Tonya the other. We shuffled toward the door that led out to the hallway. With their free hands, Tonya dragged the green tank of oxygen and Nancy pulled the clumsy IV stand.

Other patients and visitors watched the unlikely trio wobble down the hall. They gave us plenty of room. I had the feeling that no one wanted to get entangled with this procession.

We managed to get to the end of the hall, made a left turn, and unexpectedly bumped into Lawanna and Dr. Bettye Whiteaker, a friend from Dallas.

Bettye is a dentist specializing in periodontics and the wife of my former associate pastor, Kermit Whiteaker. She is a loving, caring, sensitive person. In a beautiful expression of friendship she had taken time off from her practice to be with Lawanna during my heart surgery. On this particular morning both women knew that I was trying to sleep, so they took a leisurely walk and enjoyed a late breakfast.

We hugged briefly—and very carefully—as we met in the hall. Nancy invited them to meet us in the rehabilitation room. That sounded like a good idea since there was no way five persons, a tank of oxygen, and a rickety IV stand could travel down the hall together. Lawanna and Bettye smiled at me and moved on ahead. Nancy, Tonya, and I struggled along until we reached the next wing. We reduced "speed," made a right turn, and headed for the third door on the right. With much maneuvering of the twisted, tangled tubing, we finally made it through the door.

WHAT A PICTURE!

The sight in the room held the potential of becoming the next "Norman Rockwell original" and could easily have graced the cover of any magazine. Before me sat fifteen other patients with their own "Nancy's" and "Tonya's," oxygen tanks, and makeshift portable IV stands. Spiderlike tubes connected to tanks and stands were everywhere. All fifteen patients were gasping for breath and looked as slick and pale as Johnnie Alston's hog. We resembled relics of a Civil War battlefield. The heads of at least half of those in the room slumped forward or to one side. They were sound asleep. Two or three snored. Most of the others managed to hold their heads up and their puffed eyes open, but their blank stares were hollow and haunting.

The physical therapist stood at the front of the room to welcome all the patients with a rehearsed speech. She congratulated us on making it through surgery, told us how great we looked, and assured us that our best days were ahead. She also told us that we were all going to have a "good time" for the next few minutes. Those of us who were awake doubted her words. The others couldn't have cared less. I looked around the room and envied those who slept through the welcoming address.

Then came the good news—or, so we were told. We had a choice to make. *This is great*, I thought. *This is the first time since I've been in this hospital that I've been able to make a choice. . . . about anything*.

"You can choose your own exercise," the physical therapist said sweetly. "You can either ride the exercycle for fifteen minutes, or you can walk on the treadmill for fifteen minutes."

The poor girl was hallucinating. In my condition I couldn't even climb *up* on an exercycle, let alone do fifteen minutes on one; I couldn't even take six steps on a treadmill, much less walk on one for fifteen minutes. No way!

"Which do ya' want?" Tonya commanded. Her tone ruled out any alternative options.

"I'm not sure. . . ."

"Jest make up your mind. Exercycle or treadmill?"

I sighed, "Well, I do have a treadmill at home. Maybe I can manage it a little better. But what about the oxygen tank? And I'll have to have the IV stand . . . and I'll need some help in stepping up on the treadmill."

I was building my case, certain that the obstaclcs I mentioned were greater than the challenge. Tonya disagreed.

"Here's the tank," she announced as she clattered it across half the room. "And here's the IV stand next to your left arm. Now, up we go on the treadmill," she added as she pushed the buttons and I was forced to start walking.

Fifteen minutes later I was more than exhausted; I was depleted.

Trembling. Tearful.

But at least I was aware and conscious. Some of my fellow patients had closed their eyes and fallen asleep again. One old lady slouched in a chair. Her mouth was open and drooling. She was breathing laboriously . . . snoring . . . wearing a loose fitting gown . . . legs spread wide apart . . . and totally unconcerned about her propriety and decency—or lack thereof. No one else in the room cared either.

ON THE ROAD TO RECOVERY

We had enjoyed five minutes of break time when a young, petite, attractive blonde skipped through the door and took charge of the session. She had all the marks of a fresh graduate out of training school and on her first job. She introduced herself to us as a nutritionist, and said her goal was to give advice concerning the right foods to eat and how to prepare them. I was glad Lawanna and Bettye were in the back of the room for this part of the session. I knew that Lawanna would take careful notes on everything.

The young nutritionist talked about food groups and their importance to the health of the heart. She discussed calories, fats, and cholesterol. She didn't miss a page in her textbook. The session was almost over. So was I.

She closed her notebook and made one last observation. "Now, many people ask about having sex following heart surgery. They wonder if there is any danger?"

I couldn't help but notice that those who had fallen asleep woke up instantly. Others managed to blink their eyes in bewilderment. Everyone was listening—for the first time—except the old lady in the loose gown with her legs apart.

"We've done extensive research on this," she continued demurely, "and our studies show there is no danger to the heart when having sex relations following surgery." She paused with a smile, "So when you get home and you have the urge, go right ahead and have sex with your husband or wife."

There was silence. Blank stares. The only sound in the room was the old lady snoring. Two others slumped forward in disbelief and went back to sleep.

Mustering all the strength I had left, I managed to raise my right arm.

"Yes sir, do you have a question?" she chirped with youthful enthusiasm.

"Yes ma'am," I panted for breath, while those patients who were awake perked up to listen. I mustered all the strength possible and asked in a weary, wispy voice, "Do we . . . do we *have* to?"

The therapy room instantly filled with half grunts, suppressed chuckles, and controlled "heh, heh's . . . heh, heh's." It was too painful to laugh. The nutritionist blushed slightly and looked away from the audience. Lawanna and Bettye ducked out the back door, doubled over in laughter. Nancy quickly reached for my arm, helped me out of the chair, and balanced the IV stand. Tonya pointed me toward the exit, grabbed the oxygen tank, tugged me through the door. . . .

And giggled.

THANKS, MRS. MALAPROP!

In 1775 Richard Brinsley Sheridan, an Irish-born English dramatist, wrote a play called *The Rivals*. One of the characters in the drama was a "Mrs. Malaprop" who was forever blundering in her use of words. From her comes the term "malapropism," found in the dictionary and meaning "the habit of ridiculously misusing words."

Mrs. Malaprop is alive and well today, roaming the corridors of every hospital in town. I know; I have encountered her!

"Pastor, I'm doing fine, 'cept my kidneys won't work and they had to put in this *casper.*"

"My *prostrate* is bothering me today."

"My throat is giving me trouble and the doctor says he's going to have to remove my *learnex.*"

"When we knew we were coming to the hospital we had to take care of some legal matters quickly. We didn't have time to wait, so a friend who is a judge gave us one of those *Alfred Davids.*"

"See, right there. That's where they cut the *unbiblical* cord on my baby."

"I've met some wonderful people here in the hospital—Baptists, Methodists, Episcopalians, and Catholics. But there's one group I don't understand. Would you explain the *Seventh Day Advantages* to me?"

"My heart is giving me some trouble. They're going to *cauterize* me tomorrow and put dye in my arteries."

"I'm feeling better, except for this *inner-gestion.*"

"My *hyena hernia* is acting up today."

And, then there was this little lady in deep East Texas who asked for prayer for her son during the mid-week prayer meeting. "You'all please pray for my boy," she pleaded. "You know he's a farmer. Yesterday he had an accident! He fell off his *concubine*!"

Thanks, Mrs. Malaprop. You make hospital visiting *so much more enjoyable!*

7

Growing Children

Uncle June was Mother's youngest brother and like Mother, he was born in North Carolina in a farmhouse seven miles from Siler City, five miles from Bonlee, and four miles from Bear Creek. Like all of the other Moody children, he was born at home. By the time June came along his ma and pa had almost run out of names so they asked the siblings to help. Aunt Minnie, affectionately called "Punk" by nieces and nephews in later years, gave him the name "June." It was perfectly logical, she insisted, since he was born in the month of June. So the name stuck, and "June" it was for all of his seventy-six years.

The land was poor and life was hard. From sunrise to sunset they planted, plowed, reaped, and harvested. They milked cows, raised chickens, hunted rabbits, squirrels and 'possums for food. They were poor, very poor, but so was everybody else after the turn of the century, so they didn't realize it.

June used to tell me that he and "the old mule would work all summer so the old mule could eat in the winter." He also said that Pa would buy an old sow (a mother pig, to you city people!) and raise a litter of piglets. He'd fatten them up and take them to Bonlee to sell them. While he was gone the ten children would stand around talking about what surprises Pa might bring home to them from the sale of the pigs. They fantasized chocolate drops, peppermint candy canes, oranges, and maybe—just maybe—a new pair of shoes. Late in the afternoon when they heard the clatter of the horse-drawn wagon cross the nearest bridge, they would run down the dirt road to see what he had brought them. The "oinks" from the back of the wagon told the story and shattered their hopes. Pa had sold the pigs and used the money to buy another old sow!

It was called "survival."

Like everyone else who struggled for survival along Tick Creek, under the shadow of Hickory Mountain, the Moodys had no money for entertainment. So to their credit, they entertained themselves—by telling stories.

The boys would lie on the long porch late in the afternoon after a hard day in the fields and swap yarns. They would laugh until they almost rolled off the porch. Later, they would pull up ten or twelve chairs around the dying embers of a fire and continue to tell stories.

THE RARE GIFT OF HUMOR

As a growing boy I listened and laughed. I didn't realize it then but this was humor in its purest form. It was not caustic, racist, offensive, or embarrassing. Neither was it comedy nor showmanship. Instead, it was the ability to look at the simple things of life and find in them a reason to smile, a cause to chuckle. And more important, it was the ability to laugh at oneself.

The Moody clan survived well on a "poor dirt" farm. The overworked soil never produced bountiful crops, and poverty and riches were still measured by sows and piglets.

But they laughed and lived and loved. And they kept telling their stories until the last Moody—my mother—died at the age of ninety-four.

Uncle June became a policeman in my home town, Siler City, and a few years later he was made police chief. Respectfully, I'm sure there must have been some who knew more about the technicalities of the legal system, but no policeman knew more about people and life than June Moody.

I believe this is called "wisdom."

Several years ago Uncle June moved into a new house in a wooded area of my home town. Aunt "Bea" of "Mayberry RFD" lived two or three houses up the street from him. June, a man of the earth, worked hard putting in his new lawn. He cultivated the ground and sowed seeds for grass. The grass would peep through the soil and then be trampled down by neighborhood kids, ages five or six, who played baseball in his yard. To their delight the Chief of Police loved them, encouraged them, and played with them. Before long the children were ringing his doorbell, asking if "Chief" could come out and play with them. A few weeks later "Chief" became their coach.

Almost every afternoon the gang would gather for batting practice, or to learn how to slide into second base or to chase fly balls hit to them by "Chief," who was now their "coach."

When baseball season was over the cycle would begin again. June would seed the lawn, green grass would peep through the rich soil, only to be trampled down in the coming weeks of play.

An impatient neighbor watched this cycle for two or three years. Finally in exasperation, she exclaimed, "Mr. Moody, don't you know you can't grow grass with all those children playing in your yard?"

Uncle June thought for a moment, then answered: "Lady, we can grow grass anytime; *right now we're growing children.*"

"SIC 'EM, BEARS!"

So much is involved in "growing children," as Uncle June put it. Just like "big boys and girls," they nurse their hurts and aches and they bandage their cuts and bruises (granddaughter Emily calls them "owies;" granddaughter Ali calls them "boo-boos").

And they struggle with their own disappointments and rejections. Their little bodies have a thousand (no, ten thousand!) receptacles picking up everything they see and hear and sense. These "messages received" are often returned in spontaneous, uninhibited, and sometimes unlikely ways.

For instance, Emily's parents Shannon and George are graduates of Baylor University. Like most Baylor grads they are avid, sometimes fanatical, supporters of the "Baylor Bears." Emily has attended Baylor University football games since she was a toddler. Happily, she's been so absorbed in the theatrics—marching bands, cheerleaders, and live bears—she hasn't known or worried about the scores. May her childhood innocence continue!

When she was three years old, she came home one day from Sunday school, sat down in her high chair to eat her lunch, and volunteered to sing her "new song:"

> Zacchaeus was a wee little man,
> A wee little man was he;
> He climbed up in a sycamore tree
> The Savior for to see.
> And when the Savior came that way
> He looked up in the tree and said . . .
> Sic 'em, Bears!

We think she learned most of the song in Sunday school. However, we have no idea where she learned her theology!

OUT OF THE MOUTHS OF BABES

Paul Cox, then five years of age, wondered about his pastor's theology one Sunday morning. He was seated near the front with his parents, Carolyn and Byron. I was "preaching away," as they sometimes say, exhorting people to a deeper understanding of God and to a stronger commitment to Him and to His church. In an attempt to sound profound, I paused, leaned forward over the pulpit, and raised a rhetorical question: "And God—who is God?"

In the hush of that moment Paul looked up at Byron and asked loudly enough to be heard by half the congregation, "GREAT DAY, DAD, DOESN'T *HE* KNOW?

CONFERENCE WITH A SIX-YEAR-OLD

Blair Miles was my six-year old little friend who talked like an adult.

"Bruce," he asked after church one Sunday, "could I have a conference with you?"

Blair, like most of the children in our church, called me by my first name. This wasn't something that I tried to "program;" it just happened, and it stuck. Of course, uneasy parents at first corrected the children and tried to steer them toward "Dr. McIver" (does he give shots?), or "Reverend McIver" (there were times when I didn't feel like a "reverend"), or "Brother McIver" (does that make Lawanna "Sister McIver"?). Interestingly, the parents would reprimand their child for not "showing proper respect," but before long both the parents and the child would be back to calling me "Bruce." I took this as a compliment, a special kind of bonding.

"Of course, Blair," I replied, "I'd be happy to visit with you anytime."

"First let me talk to my parents and see when they can bring me to your office," he suggested. "I'll give you a call. Thanks."

The six-year-old then shook hands with me and walked away with the demeanor of a bank president who had just closed a deal. I smiled and wondered, *What's on his mind? Maybe he wants to see my cane collection—canes from all over the world. Or, maybe he wants a closer look at the framed photograph of the Middle East taken on one of the first space flights. On the other hand, maybe he just wants to see where I sit and work.*

Three days later Blair sat in my office. He came straight to the point.

"I have a question to ask you," he began.

"Fine, Blair, what's your question?"

"How did that hole get in the sky?"

"I beg your pardon," I stammered in uncertainty.

"Well, Bruce, you remember it says in the Bible when Jesus was baptized "the heavens opened."

I gulped.

He continued, "What I want to know is how did that hole get there?"

SPEECHLESS—AGAIN!

My silence was deafening. I had read this passage in Matthew's Gospel hundreds of times through the years. I had preached on it. I had read commentaries about it and had listened to professors in the seminary discuss it. But I had never dealt with how the hole in the sky got there; neither had anyone else that I knew!

Blair waited patiently for my answer. There wasn't a hint of his trying to be cute, or "uppity," as they used to say when I was a boy in North Carolina. Blair's question was genuine. Thankfully, even though I had no definitive answer at the moment, I did have enough sense to refrain from a pat on the head and a "there, there, son, that's a big question for a little boy."

Whatever I did manage to say seemed to satisfy Blair for the moment. Then I made my big mistake.

"Now, Blair, do you have any other questions you want to ask me?"

Dumb. Big-time dumb.

"Yes, Bruce, how did Jesus walk on water?"

Gulp again.

I squirmed and coughed, wondering how I could give an answer to a perceptive child, or to an adult for that matter, without using theological jargon or pious verbiage.

Blair sensed my discomfort. "That's OK, Bruce; I guess if He could *make* the water He could walk on it."

In that moment a child became my teacher.

By the way, didn't Jesus say, "Unless you change and become like little children, you will never enter the kingdom of heaven" (Matt. 18:3 NIV)?

ANDREW'S AMAZING UNDER-THE-PEW INVESTIGATION

One Sunday morning in my sermon I pleaded with the congregation to use their minds as well as their hearts in Christian living (my visit with Blair Miles probably inspired this message). "Think!" I exhorted enthusiastically, "the Bible tells us, 'Love the Lord your God with all your heart and with all your soul and with all your mind'" (Matt. 22:37 NIV).

Throughout the congregation I saw individuals nodding. Admittedly, a simple "reality check" would have probably indicated that some of these were nodding sleepily, but most preachers who are struggling to communicate will take any kind of a nod! I did, and railed on.

"Ladies and Gentlemen," I exclaimed loudly, "you don't come into a worship service, sit down on a plush cushion, unscrew your head, and place it under the pew!"

When the service was over a concerned mother waited to speak to me in the foyer of the sanctuary. Clinging to her hand and leaning against her body was five-year-old Andrew, obviously tired and worn out.

"Pastor, I do hope my child didn't disturb you while you were preaching today."

"No," I replied warmly, "I wasn't aware of any distraction."

"You probably couldn't see it," she continued, "since we were near the back of the sanctuary."

"What happened?" I asked quietly.

"Well, after you talked about "unscrewing heads and putting them under the pews," Andrew became very fidgety. He just wouldn't sit still. I tried hard to concentrate on your message and to do what you asked us to do—think. But while I was thinking," she continued, "Andrew somehow got off the pew and began crawling around under it."

"Don't worry about that," I reassured her with a smile. "Children often get restless in a worship service."

"But he wasn't restless," she said with a wry smile.

"What was he doing?" I asked.

"Pastor, that's exactly what I leaned over and asked him."

"And?"

"And he said, *"I'm looking for heads!"*"

POSTSCRIPT

You're right, Uncle June.

"We can grow grass any time; right now we're growing children."

And they're "growing" us!

8

A Profile in Courage?

"Pastor, this is Alfred. I realize it's late but could you come to our house right now? Please?"

I recognized the high-pitched voice even though I had known Alfred for only a few weeks. The voice was one of Alfred's distinctive physical characteristics, along with a tall, lanky body and nervous eyes that darted in unpredictable patterns when he talked with you. This time the voice bounced between the obvious note of anxiety and the more subtle whine of "poor me."

"It's Ernestine," he rattled on. "I can't do a thing with her. The police have been out once tonight and I thought we had her calmed down, but—'scuse me for a minute, Pastor."

There was a pause, followed by loud crashing sounds.

"You gotta come quick," Alfred shouted, "she's throwing all the furniture out the windows and out the back door. Hurry! Please!"

On the drive across the city to their house, I shook my head as I recalled a recent conversation with a layman who had no idea what a minister did.

"It's a real world out there," he had insisted. "It's a tough world, Pastor. You'd be surprised at some of the things you'd find out there."

As I continued the drive, I glanced at my watch and saw that it was two o'clock in the morning. In a strange, twisted way I wished for the layman who tried to tell me about a "real world out there."

Then I chuckled and said out loud, "Lord, if it gets any more *real* than this, deal me out." I drove on, confident that the Lord understood my feelings.

I pulled into the driveway at Alfred's house, got out of the car, and stumbled over broken chairs and tables. The entire backyard looked like it had been hit by a Texas tornado. Shattered stuff was everywhere.

"I told you, Pastor," Alfred whimpered as he tried to clear a path for me, "I told you she was tearing everything up."

"Where is she?" I asked.

CHECK ALL GUNS AT THE DOOR

"She's upstairs with the door closed and I think," he added with a whisper, "she's got a gun."

"This is serious," I observed, followed by a haunting feeling that I had just uttered quite an understatement.

"Now, Pastor, I want you to go talk to her," Alfred begged.

"Why don't *you* go talk to her?" I asked hopefully.

"Because she might shoot me but she won't shoot you; you're a 'man of God.'"

Alfred's theological interpretation of the situation was no comfort to me—none at all. I didn't feel much like a 'man of God' as I crept hesitantly up the steps, calling gently, "*Ernestine, Ernestine.*" On the contrary, I felt very vulnerable, very fragile.

After what seemed like half an eternity she finally opened the door and walked slowly down the steps toward me. I breathed for the first time in two minutes when I saw that she didn't have the gun.

The "drama" was over for the moment, and we sat down among the debris and talked and prayed. Then we picked up broken pieces of furniture.

A week later I received another call from Alfred. "Pastor, I need you to come to our house this evening. . . ."

"Are you still having problems, Alfred?"

"No, its not that. Things are much better and . . . well, Pastor . . . we'd like to join your church."

"You want to do *what?*" I asked incredulously.

"You see, Pastor, I've been calling you 'pastor' for several weeks and we're not even members of your church. Ernestine and I have been talking about it and we want to be baptized. Can you visit with us?"

Normally a call like this would excite any minister, but I had a sinking feeling the minute I hung up the phone. I just wasn't sure about my new "converts."

Later that evening I met with them and did everything I knew to help them re-think their decision. I suggested that it might be good for them to visit other churches and get to know other ministers. I stressed the long-range significance of the commitment they were considering and reminded them that it should not be taken lightly. I played for time.

"Don't rush into this," I said in what I hoped was a calm, caring voice. "You may feel differently in the weeks to come. Besides," I continued, "you can make your own commitment in your heart, just between you and God, and you can think about baptism later."

I realized this was "evangelism-in-reverse," but I left their house that evening feeling, almost thankfully, that I had talked them out of making a public decision—at least, for now.

BUT I COULDN'T TALK THEM OUT OF IT . . .

I discovered my tactics had failed when the following Sunday morning they came down the aisle during the singing of the closing hymn and requested membership.

The congregation rejoiced; I whimpered.

In the ensuing weeks I visited with them, talked with them, prayed with them, and read the Bible with them. I did everything I knew to make sure they were prepared for baptism.

"We're ready, Pastor!" Alfred exclaimed one day after an extended visit. "We're ready to be baptized." Ernestine nodded in agreement.

I left their house that night, sighed gratefully, and thought, "Maybe . . . just maybe . . . I've seen another miracle out there in the 'real world.'"

The physical preparations were made. The baptistery was filled with water, the instructions were given, and those assisting in the baptismal service were in place. The organ music played softly and the lights dimmed. A reverent hush settled over the entire congregation.

I baptized Ernestine first. There was an angelic look on her face as she came down into the water dressed in a white robe. My heart skipped a beat. Miracles really do happen! In my most serious ministerial tone I quoted from Romans, "Buried with Christ by baptism into death," and then lowered her briefly under the water. "Raised to walk in newness of life!" I proclaimed as I lifted her out of the water.

It was a beautiful moment—one that makes the work of the ministry worthwhile.

Ernestine moved up the steps on her way to the women's dressing room. I turned in the opposite direction, smiled at Alfred, and nodded for him to enter the water. By now I was not only feeling good about the baptisms; I was delighted.

Alfred reached the center of the pool, turned around (just as I had instructed), folded his hands over his chest (as I had instructed), and closed his eyes in prayerful contemplation. I raised my right hand high (as I had been instructed as a young student in seminary) and paused for effect.

What a beautiful, moving picture for the congregation! Dimmed lights and soft organ music, white robes and gentle stirrings of the waters, personal commitments and public affirmations—all symbolizing "newness of life."

By now Ernestine had reached the top step and was out of view of the congregation. She was met there by a gracious lady, a faithful member of our church who had volunteered to assist in the service. The lady smiled warmly, handed her a dry towel, and suggested in a soft voice, "Perhaps you'd like to stand here for a moment and watch your husband be baptized."

As the organ played softly, as Alfred closed his eyes and prepared to go under the water, and as I held my right hand high toward heaven, a voice from the top step on the women's side shrilled loudly . . .

"I HOPE HE DROWNS!"

CHARIOTS OF FIRE

It was our last night in London before catching an early morning flight back to the States. I wanted it to be special—a memorable climax to a perfect "holiday," as our British friends would say. I also wanted it to be a time when we could say a special thanks to our hostess for the visit, Beryl Goodland.

"Beryl, you've been wonderful to all of us," I remarked as we stood in Trafalgar Square in the heart of London. "This is your night. We'll eat anywhere you wish; and we'll do our best, even at this late hour, to find tickets to any play you want to see in the theater tonight."

Lawanna nodded her head in agreement; so did Wendell and Margaret Cook. Wendell, a petroleum engineer consultant, was chairman of the deacon fellowship back in Dallas and Margaret was a leader in the many mission activities sponsored through our church. The three of us, plus twenty others, had spent several days in Gorsley where Beryl's husband, Pat, served as pastor. Gorsley is a quaint village in the rural part of England, located eighty miles west of London and ten miles from the border of Wales. It has a school, a pub, and a church. Lawanna and I had discovered on previous visits that some of the most wonderful people in the world live there. Pat and Beryl, our good friends for years, had also found wonderful people in Dallas on their visits with us. This interchange of friendships led to the idea of a "link up," as Pat described it, between our two churches.

While in Gorsley we lived in the homes of the people. There were no hotels, but 400-year-old houses proved to be better than the most luxurious inns anywhere. We strolled down narrow lanes with our new friends, exchanged ideas and shared experiences, and drank a barrel of tea and ate a bushel of scones around their tables. We sang and worshipped in their church and in their homes. Walls of inhibition came tumbling down and to everybody's surprise, we laughed together. Perceptions of Texans garnered from television's *Dallas* died a natural death with our new friends. They expressed delight that we were not all like the disdainful "J. R.," and were surprised that some of our group had never been to "Southfork." And, our impressions about proper and staid Britons were soon forgotten in warm hospitality and hugs of friendship.

After our visit in Gorsley, Beryl graciously escorted our group on a coach tour through Wales, the Lake District of England, and the Highlands of Scotland. When we reluctantly returned to the snarled traffic and din of London, most of the people from Dallas scattered for a free evening on their own. Lawanna and I welcomed the opportunity of a last visit with Beryl before leaving the next morning. Happily, Margaret and Wendell had also joined us. The four of us wanted to express added thanks to Beryl for the tour that she had arranged and for her special "touches" as the tour guide.

So . . .

AN UNEXPECTED PLEASURE

"Beryl, this last night is yours," I said. "Name your favorite restaurant and the theater you'd like to attend."

She hesitated for a moment and then said, "There's a good Chinese restaurant just around the corner in Picadilly Circus. It's not far from here."

"Great!" I replied. "We'll eat there."

"And," she added after another pause, "there's a new movie that's been made about a friend of mine—a missionary who was in China when my family and I were there. I hear the film is rather good," she continued in her distinct British accent. "I think I would like to see it if we can still get tickets."

"That's fine, Beryl," I responded with a forced lilt in my voice, hoping to disguise the disappointment I felt.

For heaven's sake, I thought. *Our last night in London and we end up going to see some low-budget, second-rate religious movie about a missionary who served in China forty years ago!* But I had given my word to my friend and I intended to keep it, painful as the experience might be. What did she mean, "if we can still get tickets?" *Surely*, I almost laughed to myself, *anyone in London can get tickets to some unheard of movie about missionaries in China*.

As we finished our dinner Wendell looked at his watch and volunteered, "I'll go now and pick up the tickets so you folks won't have to wait in line."

Line? I thought. *What line?*

We thanked him, and he was on his way. Lawanna, Beryl, Margaret, and I had another cup of tea and waited . . . and waited. During the wait Beryl talked softly, remembering her friend about whom the movie had been made.

"He was a great runner," she said, "and one of our greatest heroes. He was from Scotland where I lived as a child with my family before my parents went to China as missionaries. In the 1924 Olympic Games he was Britain's hope for the 100 meter race, and our nation's only hope for its first gold medal. The trial heats were scheduled for Sunday and Eric had strong Christian convictions about racing on Sunday. So he withdrew from the race. It created quite a sensation, both in Paris where the Olympics were being held and back here in England. The Olympic Committee and some of the national leaders tried to get him to relent, but he stood by his convictions."

"Later," she continued, "he decided to enter the 400 meter race and to everyone's surprise, he won by five meters, setting a new world record and bringing home our nation's first gold medal ever." They called him 'The Flying Scotsman.' You may have heard of him."

I hadn't—but I was fascinated with the story. I was also deeply moved by the way Beryl talked about the athlete. I sensed that there was more here than winning races and bringing home medals. Much more.

"A year after he won the gold medal," she added, "he surprised everyone by announcing that he was going to the Shantung province of China as a missionary. Hundreds saw him off at Waverly station in London and he led them in singing, "Jesus Shall Reign Where'er The Sun."

"What did he do in China?" I asked.

"He taught science in a middle school and directed the athletic program. He did this for several years until . . ."

"Until what?" I asked.

"Until the Japanese invaded China and he was arrested. He was sent to the Weihsien Concentration Camp, one hundred miles inland, where my parents, my two brothers, my sister, and I were also imprisoned. There were 1,400 of us including 500 children, crowded into the camp. I was about twelve years of age."

"How long were you in the concentration camp?" I asked, oblivious to the time and to others around us.

"Three years," she replied. "But he . . . 'Uncle' Eric . . . made life better for us. He was always full of life, always smiling and laughing. He organized races and games for everyone, taught science, and tutored personally those who were lagging behind in their studies. He was kind and good."

I was ready with another question as Wendell walked through the door, smiling and holding up four tickets. "The last in the house for the late show," he beamed. "I had to stand in a line nearly a block long to get these."

Promptly at nine o'clock we crowded through the doors with hundreds of others as the theme song of *Chariots of Fire* reverberated throughout the theater. The lights dimmed and we watched the opening scene of a young athlete running on the beach. Lawanna was seated on my right; Beryl was on my left.

The music swelled and my heart pounded with every note. The young man on the screen threw back his head and ran faster and faster in unorthodox style. His arms were in perpetual motion, flapping by his side, and his knees were lifted higher with every stride. There was laughter on his face and he ran with reckless, joyful abandonment.

I turned to express my excitement with Beryl and noticed tears trickling down her face. Then she whispered above the music, "That's him! That's him! They've captured his personality on film!"

My own emotions ran the gamut the next two hours—joy, laughter, tears, and celebration. And gratitude, too, for sitting beside the one person in the theater who could understand and experience fully *Chariots of Fire*.

I limped out of the theater, emotionally and physically drained.

A week later I stood in the pulpit at Wilshire in Dallas and said, "I don't normally use this time to recommend movies. But, I saw one in London last week that was the most inspiring I've ever seen. Now, I doubt that it will ever make it to Dallas," I added, "but if it does, don't miss it."

I was wrong. It made it to Dallas, and to all of America. And six months after I had "experienced" it in London, *Chariots of Fire* won the Oscar for the best picture of the year.

THE REST OF THE STORY

In the ensuing years Beryl Goodland has pieced together other facets of the story. I never tire of hearing it.

After arriving in China, the "hero of Great Britain" met and married the daughter of other missionaries. Two daughters were born to the happy couple. As tensions increased between China and Japan, Eric Liddell sent his wife and girls to Canada, her native country, for safety. A third daughter was born soon after his wife arrived back home.

When Pearl Harbor was attacked on December 7, 1941, Eric was put under house arrest and later sent to the Weihsien Concentration Camp.

On February 21, 1945, the one who once made headlines around the world because of his convictions died in a crowded, bed-bug infested concentration camp—because of those same convictions. Forty-three years of age. Brain tumor.

He never held his third daughter or lived to see his family again.

Beryl Goodland, then fifteen years of age, served as a member of the honor guard as his body was removed from the camp. The next day she wrote in her diary:

> "Dear Uncle Eric died last night. It was so sudden. He wrote a letter to his wife just that day. Everyone was greatly impressed. I feel so sorry for her. Most people said he was the best man in the camp. What a loss! It snowed today. There was no coal."

POSTSCRIPT

Three months after returning from England I received a telephone call from Dan Vestal, then pastor of the First Baptist Church, Midland, Texas.

"Bruce," he said, "I have a friend in California who is interested in distributing a film in America. It's a good film—made in England—about an Olympic runner. My friend would like to have a private showing in Dallas to see how much interest there would be in the film. Would you help by telling some of your friends and contacts about the showing? By the way, I think they call it *Chariots of . . .*"

"Where are you now, Dan?" I interrupted.

"In my office."

"Standing or sitting?"

"Standing."

"Sit down, Dan; I want to tell you a story. . . ."

And I did.

9

Both Sides of the Coin

Alone. . . .

After fifteen years I am still unable to erase the picture of the young man from my mind. I first saw him as he stood silhouetted in the door of my study, obviously a shadow of what once was. The coat of his stylish conservative business suit draped loosely like a shroud over his shoulders. His perfectly matched tie and oversized shirt accentuated his thin, sunken face. His hands trembled slightly and his hollow eyes reflected fear. I did not know him nor to my knowledge had I ever seen him.

"Pastor, could I talk with you for a moment?" he asked hesitantly.

"Of course," I answered as reassuringly as possible. "Have a seat."

He walked across the study with some effort, steadying himself first on a conference table, then holding to the back of a chair. Everything about his presence indicated he had a serious medical problem.

"How can I help?" I asked, hoping the question itself would open a door of understanding.

"I just need a friend," he replied. "I'm a very sick person."

"Well, we'll get on that right away. I'm a trustee of one of the medical centers here in Dallas and we have one of the best facilities anywhere in the world. Many of the physicians on staff there are my friends; in fact, several are members right here at Wilshire. I'll get on the phone and make some calls immediately and . . ."

"No, Pastor, that won't work."

"What do you mean, it won't work? You need help and resources are available. We'll line up the best doctors . . ."

"No, Pastor," he interrupted again. "It just won't work."

"Well, if it's a matter of money," I suggested benevolently, "I'm sure something can be worked out. We have some limited funds here at the church for people in need and I'm sure the business office at the hospital will work with us. The important thing is to get you some help as soon as possible."

"It's too late," he said, shaking his head. "I've seen a dozen doctors elsewhere, and I've been through all the tests and several surgical procedures. There's no medical hope."

No hope, I thought. *In a city with one of the world's leading medical schools, several medical centers pioneering in areas of research, dozens of other excellent hospitals, and hundreds of physicians and medical support persons . . . no hope?*

NO OPTIONS—ONLY CHRIST

The young man read my thoughts and said again, "There's no hope. I have no more options."

By now I began to hear him and believe him, difficult as it was. Then searching for other means of support for him, I said, "Tell me about your family. How are they handling this?" "I moved to Dallas two years ago from West Texas," he offered. "My family knows about my illness but they have rejected me. We have no contact."

"What on earth do you mean?" I protested. "Are you telling me that they're not standing with you in this situation?"

He lowered his head and said with resignation, "I haven't heard from them in a year. They asked me not to call them again."

My emotions began to bounce from compassion to empathy, from concern to anger. He observed this non-professional display silently. Then he slowly and painfully rose from his seat, walked over to the window, stared outside for a long minute, and then quietly asked, "Do you think I could join this church? I'd like to get this one last thing settled before . . ."

We prayed together and embraced. He smiled and moved slowly out the door, leaving me to wrestle with my own confusion and bewilderment.

The following Sunday after my sermon we sang a "hymn of commitment," as was our custom. I encouraged any who wished to make a public affirmation of faith or join the church to meet me at the front as we sang. He struggled to walk down the aisle and greeted me as though he were "coming home." The congregation warmly greeted him.

Two weeks later I received word that he was in a hospital in a suburban area of the city. I planned to visit him the next day, then learned that he was no longer a patient there. He left no forwarding address.

Oh, well, I rationalized. *He's probably moved to a new apartment complex. Dallas is a big city and people are always moving around.* But I never could locate him and I never saw him in a worship service again.

Four years later I was in the office of a physician-friend. In the course of conversation we talked about a new disease that crippled the immune system and inevitably caused death. The physician then shared almost incidentally that two of his friends had been among the first doctors in Dallas to treat patients with this disease.

"In what hospital did they practice?" I inquired.

"Bradford Community," he replied. "I knew them and their work because soon after medical school I worked in the emergency room at Bradford at nights. It helped pay the bills."

I didn't respond and he looked at me with a puzzled expression, "Why do you ask?"

The wheels in my mind were turning and I spoke haltingly, "There was a young man . . . came to see me . . . joined our church . . . entered Bradford . . . said there was no hope . . ."

I then mentioned his name.

"I remember him," my physician-friend responded somberly. "I remember him well."

"How is he?" I asked eagerly. "Where is he?"

"He died that night. Never made it out of ER."

"What happened? What was wrong with him?"

"Acquired Immune Deficiency Syndrome."

AIDS.

When the shock subsided I managed to whisper the question, "Was anyone with him? His family?"

"No," the physician quietly said. "That's one reason I remember him. He died alone."

Alone.

FAMILY VALUES

The telephone rang before dawn one morning and I rolled over sleepily and grappled for the receiver. "Probably another crank call," I muttered to myself, or worse still, the "ex" of that fellow with a name similar to mine who had once lived in Dallas and who seemed to have gone underground. After taking "wrong numbers" for him all through the day and at weird hours during the night, I was convinced life would have been simpler for me if the other "Bruce" had lived in another city; or if he had just paid his bills and stayed home!

But the call early that morning was not for the phantom "Bruce," but for "Pastor."

I recognized the voice of the caller immediately—a young man who had attended graduate school in our city and had been a faithful member of our church in the process. It had been four years since his graduation and move to another state, but I remembered him fondly and gratefully.

"Joe, what on earth are you doing calling this early in the morning?" I asked with a teasing chuckle. And then I added, "You know I'm not a morning person. How are things in South Carolina? And how in the world are you?"

"I'm in Dallas, Pastor, and I'm sick—very sick."

"Sick? What happened? Where are you staying?"

In a weak, slurred speech he mumbled just above a whisper, "I came here yesterday for a conference, became ill last night, and was brought to the hospital by friends attending the conference . . . emergency . . . very weak . . . loss of body fluids."

He paused to catch his breath and continued, "I'm so sick . . . can't even get out of bed by myself. And I'm scared. They won't tell me much . . . just keep running tests on me."

"What can I do, Joe? Say the word and I'm on the way."

"I need you, Pastor," he pleaded. "And I need Lawanna. Could the two of you please come to the hospital now?"

Twenty minutes later we were on the way and forty minutes later we walked into his room. I was totally unprepared for what we found. His emaciated body, racked by pain, trembled as he reached out to take our hands. A tear trickled down his cheek as he labored and panted for strength to speak.

There are moments when words are unnecessary, when merely uttering them violates the significance of "presence." This was such a moment, so we simply held hands and cried with him.

When he gained enough composure to speak, he looked at us with pleading eyes and asked, "Would you please help me to the bathroom? Do you mind? I don't have enough strength."

Lawanna put her hands behind his back and gently lifted him off the pillow while I guided his thin legs toward the edge of the bed. We braced him while he sat in that position for a moment. Every movement, every action was a painful, exhausting struggle.

He paused to catch his breath and with a groan made an effort to stand on wobbly legs. He then draped an arm around the shoulders of each of us and shuffled in uncertainty, step by stumbling step, across the room.

The return trip was even more painful and exhausting and he collapsed in fatigue across the bed. Again, no one spoke for several minutes. Words were not needed, and they required more energy that any of us had.

He dozed while Lawanna and I looked at each other in concern. An eerie silence filled the room.

A TERRIBLE DIAGNOSIS

The brief respite was broken as two white-coated physicians opened the door and walked in and stood on either side of the bed. They nodded briefly to us and said to the sleepy young man, "Joe, the tests don't look good. We've been checking them all night and they just don't look good. Not at all."

"What are you trying to tell me?" Joe asked in confusion as Lawanna and I inched closer to the doctors.

"What's wrong? What do I have?" Joe pleaded.

"Your immune system has shut down and to further complicate matters, you have a severe case of pneumonia. Both lungs are involved and you have nothing left to fight the virus."

The other physician struck the final blow, "We're sorry, but it looks like you have . . . AIDS."

Stunned silence. Absolute silence.

"Where did I get this?" Joe whimpered.

"We don't know," one answered. "Your medical records indicate you had a vaccine in the Far East. Could have been a contaminated needle. Could have been something else," he added as his voice trailed off. "But our main concern now is to try to make you as comfortable as possible."

"Give it a few days," the other added as they moved from the bedside, "and you might be strong enough to return to South Carolina."

With that they slowly walked out and closed the door behind them. They were neither rude nor curt; there just wasn't anything else to say.

Lawanna, Joe, and I were left to ourselves in an empty room—a tomb. Prisoners to lab reports. Shattered. Isolated.

"My parents were called last night," Joe said. "They'll be arriving most any time. I can't tell them." He looked at me with a new kind of pain written across his face.

"I'll tell them," I offered.

"And someone needs to call Janice. Could you . . .?" he asked as he looked at Lawanna.

"I'll try," Lawanna replied, choking back the tears and wondering how she could break the news to Joe's lovely wife who was expecting their first child any day.

Two hours later the parents arrived and came to Joe's room for a brief visit. They were surprised, even shocked, to find him so sick, but they assured him of their love and told him not to worry about the finances or anything else. "We'll get you strong," the father said with a forced smile, "and we'll have you home in no time at all."

After a brief prayer they left to find a hotel room. I followed them out and asked them to walk with me to the "family room."

"It's private there," I volunteered, "and we can have a few minutes to visit without interruption." I tried to make the invitation sound as natural as possible, but I was trembling deep down inside.

When we reached the room we were joined unexpectedly by the primary physician on Joe's case. I welcomed his presence.

"Mr. and Mrs. Harris, I'm afraid I have some bad news for you," he said, getting straight to the point.

A look of shock registered on their faces. "What do you mean?" The father asked.

"Your son has AIDS."

"AIDS? Are you sure? Maybe there's been a mix-up in the lab studies. Not AIDS."

"AIDS, Mr. Harris. AIDS. I'm sorry."

SURROUNDED BY LOVE

"How long does he have?" the father asked in a broken voice.

"There's no way we can predict that. If we can get him over this pneumonia, maybe a year . . . maybe six months. But that's really out of our hands."

"I understand," the father replied with difficulty while the mother wept quietly.

After expressions of concern and offers to do all he possibly could, the physician slipped out of the room.

Once again—twice in one morning—an overwhelming sense of eerie silence. Before me sat two good, simple, God-fearing people from a rural village in a distant state. Their world had been shattered in less than two minutes. Life would never be the same again. They were dealing with an ominous disease that few people at the time, including the best researchers, knew anything about. But they were also dealing with a disease that many people, including preachers, had no hesitation talking about freely and pompously, amplifying all the stigmas involved.

In the eerie silence of that "family room" I pondered all this with anger, and compassion, and questions.

What would the parents do? How would they react? What would they tell their neighbors? Their fellow church members? Their pastor?

Finally, mustering all the courage I had at the moment, I asked, "How will you deal with this?" In some ways it was a dumb question; in other ways it struck at the very heart of their lives.

There was a pause, and then the father reached for his wife's hand. He stroked it gently and then held it in a spirit of divine togetherness.

In a clear, resolute voice he said, "We'll take him home with us, hug him tight, and love him until he dies."

They did.

A year later I stood by Joe's grave, joined hands with his family, and sang "Amazing Grace."

POSTSCRIPT

Two stories. Two lives touching my ministry. Two families. Two sets of "family values."

"Alone."

And, "We'll take him home, hug him tight, and love him until he dies."

10

All in the Family

After Dad died, Mother—affectionately called "Mommie Mac"—stubbornly insisted she could and would live her own life in her own house, relying on her own resources. Her fierce spirit of independence caused family members to smile in tolerance and wring hands in frustration. She would not move and she would not *be* moved!

"Thank you for your offers," she said repeatedly, "but I'd rather just live in my own house. Besides, I don't want to give up my things."

Her "things" included her own bed, a refrigerator and stove, some special pictures on the walls, a reading chair and large print Bible, and a few magazines and the daily newspaper (she always read the obituary column first), dresser drawers packed with family memorabilia, and a stray cat that hung around the back door. "Things" also included an eighteen-inch statue of "Rebekah at the Well" that had graced our parlor since I was a little boy. Mother had purchased the "gold-trimmed" figurine from a traveling salesman and had paid for it out of her egg money. As a child I had no idea who Rebekah was. I certainly didn't know that she had married the biblical Isaac, Abraham's son, but I got the idea early on that she was somebody very special and that the statue was not to be handled by children.

One of her "things" that made us all nervous was a step-stool in the kitchen.

Mommie Mac used it daily, either sitting on the padded top while drying dishes or climbing on it while searching for things in shelves high above the cabinets.

"Mother, please don't do that!" we pleaded. "Don't climb on the stool or on any other piece of furniture. You'll break your leg." She tuned us out.

Niece Susan even made a sign and taped it on the stool: "STAY OFF! THIS MEANS YOU, MOMMIE MAC!" She adored Susan, but she ignored the sign.

MOTHER'S INDEPENDENCE

Once on a trip back home, I walked into the kitchen and found her on the third step of the stool reaching for something on the top shelf, swaying back and forth while trying to maintain her balance. My heart skipped a beat and I gasped under my breath. Fearing that I might startle her, I swallowed hard, lowered my voice,and coaxed as calmly as possible, "Please, Mother, get down . . . slowly. I don't want you to fall." It was the same tone of voice I had used when I once called Renie, then about four years of age, to come "straight into the house and stop hugging that dog"—a strange Great Dane that had wandered into our front yard.

"He won't hurt me," Renie had responded as both her chubby arms encircled the neck of the huge dog, "he's my friend."

Mother's response was about the same as Renie's.

"Mother," I begged after her awkward, but successful, descent, "Don't ever do that again. I'm not going back to Texas until you promise me that you will never climb up on that stool again."

She reacted like a little child caught in the very act of something.

"I'm serious, Mother. I want you to promise me now, on your word, that you will stay off that stool. I'm asking this for your own good and for my peace of mind."

"Well, all right," she conceded while looking down at the floor. "All right, if you insist, I promise."

Then she looked up at me with a devilish twinkle in her eyes and added, "I promise I won't climb up there any more . . . unless . . .," she added with an impish grin, "unless there's something up there I really need."

I gave up. Thankfully, Mommie Mac survived step-stools. But watermelons and peaches did her in.

She could eat half a watermelon by herself, and often did. Then she'd stash the other half in the refrigerator and save it for the next day. She would do the same thing with fresh peaches. She'd buy a bushel, peel half of them for canning, and eat the rest. Her appetite was great; her nutritional balance was terrible. When her blood count dropped dangerously low, a hurried decision was made for her to move to Greensboro and live with my sister, Ella, a nurse and an administrator of a retirement center. It took a lot of talking on our part but Mother finally agreed and the doors to the white bungalow were locked. The forty-mile move was made in one day; the transition took in a lifetime.

"Annie," a fifteen-pound Boston Terrier with a pug nose and pleading black eyes, helped in the transition. Mother and Annie bonded. They ate together, walked together, and sometimes got into trouble together.

The telephone rang in Ella's office one day. Fay, the next-door neighbor, was on the line. "Now, Ella," she said, "I don't want to disturb you, but I think you should come home."

TROUBLE WITH "THE CHILDREN"

"What's the problem?" Ella asked anxiously, thinking that Mother had fallen or was ill.

"I don't know how it happened," Fay answered, "but your Mother and Annie are both locked in the dog lot in the backyard and can't get out."

Ella drove home with the key, unlocked the gate, and rescued her "children," as she called them.

One day a kind lady from my sister's church came to visit Mommie Mac. Her visit was part of a special ministry to elderly people who could not participate in the regular services of the church. As the visit concluded, the visitor suggested that the two of them might sing a hymn or a song and then have prayer together. The church visitor began singing "Jesus Loves Me" and Mother joined in. So did Annie. The three of them sang and howled through two verses, and Mother insisted proudly that Annie sang in "perfect pitch."

"I do wish I had paid more attention to Annie when she was little," Mother observed later that evening. "I do think I could have taught that dog to talk."

After a couple of broken hips it became necessary to find some help for Mommie Mac on a daily basis. This was more of a problem than anyone imagined.

Cora Mae, an oversized, elderly spinster, was the first one we tried. She made it OK for a few days—until she washed her underwear and hung it on limbs of the dogwood trees around the house, insisting "that's the reason God gave us sunshine." She achieved this by pulling the branches down with a garden rake, hooking the clothing on the branches, and then releasing the rake. Ingenious. So ingenious that neighbors stopped to stare. Blossoms look beautiful on dogwood trees in North Carolina; bloomers don't.

Janie worked as a "sitter" for about a month—until she began bringing her teenage daughter with her . . . and the two sat on the couch watching television all day while Mother cooked for them.

Others also came and went. One refused to give Mother raisins for her cereal each morning. No reason was given; she just refused. Another didn't like dogs so her days were numbered.

Then came Hilda Mae, a caring but somewhat overbearing black lay-preacher. Her presence effused piety—a piety oozing with scriptural admonitions and exhortations. One day when Mother was not feeling well, Hilda Mae urged her on.

"Now, Mommie Mac," she announced in a voice that could have filled a church house, "The Lord wants us to be HOLY; He jes' wants us to be HOLY!"

Mother ignored her for a moment as though she had not heard. It was obvious that she was in no mood for lofty exhortations and pious declarations.

"Hilda Mae," she finally said as she rolled over in the bed, "I'm not trying to be holy; I'm just trying to be *daily*."

Mommie Mac was *daily* until the day she died.

FIVE NICKELS AND A BEAR

Mommie Mac, ninety-four years of age, smiled as she opened the package that had just been delivered.

"It's just like the picture in the catalogue," she said proudly to Carol, her nurse, as she studied the silver-plated teddy bear bank. She had ordered the bank shortly after her granddaughter, Shannon, had told her that she would soon become a great-grandmother. This would be a "first" for Mommie Mac, and she was thrilled.

"Now, Carol, hand me those five new nickels we got at the bank yesterday—the ones with '1990' engraved on them."

Carol took the shiney coins from a bedside table and carefully placed them in the wrinkled and weathered hands. The elderly woman lovingly fingered a coin and hesitantly dropped it through the slot on the top of the bear's head. The "clink" of the coin signaled the completion of its journey from the head to the feet of the silver bear. It also signaled a rite of passage—the ending of one life and the beginning of another . . . a legacy from one generation to another.

Mommie Mac fondled the bear for a moment, handed it to her nurse, and observed softly, "There—those five nickles should be enough to get the baby off to a good start in life. Besides," she added with a grin, "we don't want to *spoil* the child."

Five nickels? How much is five nickels?

More than Mommie Mac ever had as a little girl at the turn of the century . . . more than the cost of an orange, an apple, and candy at Christmas . . . more than the price of a toy or a doll . . . more than the cost of twenty-five dippers of lemonade on the Fourth of July . . . or a pair of gloves . . . or a hat . . . or stockings . . . or a knife . . . or a teapot . . . or the vest-pocket edition of *Webster's Dictionary*.

Five shiney nickels—more than most any child living on a farm could imagine at the turn of the century.

"Now, Carol," she said, "I want you to take this bear and tie a nice pink ribbon around its neck."

"Do you think we should use pink?" Carol asked. "We're not sure if the baby will be a boy or a girl."

"It will be a girl," Mommie Mac announced with certainty. "No doubt about it, that baby will be a pretty little girl."

"Put the bear in a nice box and hide him away," she continued. "I won't be here when the baby is born, but I want you to make sure that my great-granddaughter gets this." And then she added with a smile of satisfaction and a characteristic twinkle in her eyes, "Don't tell anyone now; this will be our little secret."

MOMMIE MAC'S LEGACY

A month later Mommie Mac died—five months before little Emily was born. When we returned home from her funeral in North Carolina we brought with us the silver-plated bear bank containing the five new nickels. Shannon and her husband, George, placed it in their newly decorated nursery as a silent reminder of love . . . and legacy.

When Emily was two years of age, she and her "best friend," Troy, were playing in her room. Four little eyes spotted the silver bear and four little legs supporting two little bodies scurried up chairs and tables and desk tops to reach it. Shannon later found the bear toppled over, ribbon in disarray, lying on its side—empty. She picked it up and shook it. Not a single "clink" and not a single shiney nickel.

"Emily!" Shannon asked sternly, "Where are the nickels?"

"Troy . . . Troy . . ." Emily stammered with a quivering chin as she pointed toward the open door leading out of the house. Troy had made a fast exit.

"Did Troy take the nickels?"

She said as she shook her head from side to side and managed a mumbled, "No."

"Then how did he get them?" Shannon quizzed.

Emily looked at the floor and answered hesitantly as though she had done something terribly wrong, "I gave them to him."

That was several months ago. With Troy's help and with the help of his parents, three of the "1990 nickels" have been found, and they're still looking for the other two.

When I heard what had happened to the coins, I exclaimed, "Oh, no. Those nickels were picked out especially for Emily. That's a gift from a great-grandmother, no longer living, to her first great-grandchild. Why, that's a legacy . . . from one generation to another. That's the kind of gift you protect—on a very high shelf where little children can't reach it . . . or in a glass case . . . or in a dark closet."

The ensuing months and memories of my own childhood have soothed and softened my reactions.

Somewhere . . . somehow . . . I think I can hear Mommie Mac say, "Now you just hush, Son. I gave those nickels to that little girl. They're hers, not yours. If she wants to give all five of them away and if she wants to give away the bear bank also, she can do it. Now, stop fretting over something that's not yours."

The little boy in me listens . . . and answers . . . just as I was taught by benevolent parents in the hills of home, "Yes ma'am, Mother."

But Mother has not finished. "Don't you make that child feel bad about those nickels," she says. "She just wanted to be nice to her friend. You grown-ups leave those children alone."

"And, besides," she adds, "you only keep what you give away."

"Yes ma'am, Mother; yes ma'am."

LEAVING HOME

The long-awaited day had finally arrived. Renie, the youngest of our three daughters and the last one still at home, was leaving for college and I wasn't prepared for it.

Lawanna and I had watched Kathie, our oldest, drive off to Austin College; then on to Guilford College in North Carolina and finally to Greensboro College in the same state. But Kathie was the "big sister" who thrived on the academics, so her moving toward the university setting seemed the natural and appropriate thing to do. We had also watched Shannon travel a hundred miles south to enroll in Baylor University, but we knew that we would see her frequently and we also knew that one of the girls was still at home.

But that June morning of 1980 slipped up on me. I knew in my head this "rite of passage" in the McIver family was inevitable and it could lead to good, but my heart had difficulty getting the message. Was this really happening to us? Were all our children old enough to leave home? What would life be like for us with three empty bedrooms? And what would it be like for Renie? I pondered these questions as I surveyed the cluttered piles of clothing and furnishings yet to be loaded into the car. "There's not a room on the campus of Baylor University that can hold all this stuff," I chuckled out loud to no one in particular.

I pondered . . . and remembered another "leaving."

The year was 1942 . . . nearly forty years earlier. The place was Siler City, a small town located in the heart of North Carolina. I was sitting with my father at Buster Elder's Shell Service Station and Bus Stop . . . waiting . . . with a lump in my throat . . . trying to think of something to say.

"'Bout time for the bus for Asheville to come," Dad observed.

"Yep, I guess it is," I replied, swallowing hard.

"Take care of yourself, Son, and study hard."

"I will; I promise."

"Got your money?"

"Yes sir, all seventy-five dollars."

"That ought to get you started. Now if you need any more, let me know."

"Thanks, Dad."

The bus lurched around the corner and ground to a stop. We both knew, painfully, that time was up and the wait was over. I shook hands with my father and climbed on board, dragging up the steps behind me most of my worldly possessions in an old tin suitcase and a cardboard box. I placed them in the overhead luggage rack, found a seat, and waved a hesitant, awkward good-bye to Dad. Neither of us suspected as the bus slowly pulled away that the two-hundred mile trip through the Blue Ridge Mountains to Mars Hill College would two years later lead to a twelve-hundred-mile pilgrimage across the Red River and into Texas. And neither of us dreamed in that moment that the roots of my life and work would sink into the soil of another state and I would never return home again, except for all-too-brief-visits.

LETTING GO OF RENIE

But enough of this philosophizing, I thought, as I picked up one of Renie's boxes and headed toward the car in front of our house. Actually there were two cars, for there was no way that all her things could be packed into one automobile. Ingenuously, Renie had enlisted some of her friends to help her move from Dallas to Waco. She and Jana Jones had arranged to travel in Renie's faded-blue, second-hand Chevy Impala. Duncan Brooks and Doyle Knowles planned to follow them in Duncan's old Ford Mustang.

After two hours of constant work and careful juggling, both cars were crammed full of clothing and other belongings. "Leaving home" was about to become reality—if the drivers and the passengers could squeeze into the front seats.

"Just a minute!" I shouted with feigned excitement, "Let's get everyone together for a last picture."

"Great idea!" someone responded, "but we need to call Marcie and Laurie. They're swimming in the pool in the backyard." Marcie Murrell and Laurie Paschal, classmates and long-time friends of our girls, joined us in the front yard, dripping wet and dressed in skimpy bikinis. Other friends showed up out of nowhere to take part in the celebrative send-off.

Lawanna photographed the entire group and then took a picture of me writing a check and handing it to Renie. There were hugs and kisses, laughter and tears and final waves as they climbed into the cars. Lawanna and I turned and walked slowly back into our now-empty nest, pondering the adjustments before us. For more years than we had the energy to count we had been consumed by the girls' schedules: car pools, cheerleading practice, piano lessons and recitals, drill team practice, choir rehearsals, football games, retreats and camps, swim parties, and on and on. We had enjoyed these but I welcomed the adjustments.

As I closed the door and stepped into the den there was an eerie silence, as if the walls were asking, "What's happened?"

I smiled and said to Lawanna, "I'll miss all the girls but I'm looking forward to some peace and quiet around here."

Lawanna did not have time to respond. From the street came a piercing scream, "Mr. McIver! Mr. McIver!"

I dashed back out the door as someone shouted, "Duncan's car is on fire!" I looked and saw smoke billowing from under the hood of the Mustang.

WHERE THERE'S SMOKE, THERE'S FIRE

"Quick! Unload the car!" I yelled as I turned and ran back into the house.

"Lawanna, call the fire department! Duncan's car is on fire!"

"Are you sure?" she asked in bewilderment.

"Lawanna, *please* call the fire department!"

"Have you tried to smother it with . . .?"

"Now, Lawanna, NOW!"

Five minutes later the huge red fire engine careened around the corner, siren splitting the air, and stopped in the middle of the street in front of our house. Four helmeted firemen wearing yellow hip boots moved quickly and efficiently to Duncan's car, raised the hood, doused the flames and laid charred ignition wires on the ground. Their work was finished but they were gracious enough to linger to make sure that there were no other problems.

Or, they might have lingered to try to comprehend the sights before them. Clothing, lamps, books and albums, pillows, sheets, and graduation gifts littered the sidewalks and the four adjoining yards. A dozen high school students and graduates, some who had shown up to swim, wandered around in all kinds of dress, and undress on our own lawn. Neighbors came from houses up and down the block, took one look at the disarray, and shook their heads in disbelief. In the aftermath of the near-disaster, Laurie walked up to the driver of the fire engine and whispered something to him. He looked at her, scanned the crowd of students, shook his head and motioned to the other fireman that it was time to leave.

"Renie," I inquired quietly, "what did Laurie say to the fireman?"

"She asked him if he would take us all for a ride on the fire truck," she replied hesitantly.

I shook my head, looked at the scattered debris, and watched the fire engine as it chugged around the corner and said to Lawanna, "You know, Honey, I'm gonna miss all this excitement!"

POSTSCRIPT:

Thirteen years later the telephone rang. Renie, now the wife of John and the mother of Ali and "John-John," called from a distant state.

"Dad, we're all coming home for a week," she said excitedly.

"Wonderful," I responded, "what would you like to do while you're home?"

"Nothing, Dad; we just want to come home."

I thought of the hills of North Carolina . . . Buster Elder's Shell Station and Bus Stop . . . a tin suitcase . . . and a handshake. . . .

"I know what you mean," I replied softly, gratefully. "I know exactly what you mean."

NAPPINESS IS . . .

I opened the folder, removed the faded envelope, fingered it for a moment, and read the inscription: "Napoleon (Nappy) McIver, Ridge Spring Drive, Dallas, Texas."

Then I lifted the flap and studied the picture and the note inside:

> Dear Nappy:
>
> The doggie pictured on the card looks like one of my permanent resident orphans, Benny, who was one of your companions while you stayed with us. Hope you are doing well. Will be on vacation and out of town for about ten days, commencing the 19th. Give your folks my best wishes. I will get in touch with you when I return. Take care, stay out of trouble and out of the street.
>
> Your friend,
>
> Wes Porter

I laid the letter down and smiled . . . and remembered. . . .

Nappy—short for Napoleon Bonaparte—was a black miniature French poodle who thought he was a person. Over my protests he came to live with us shortly after my first open heart surgery. The girls and Lawanna insisted that I needed the companionship of a dog and that a dog "will help with the healing process," and "Dad, you need a male friend in this house filled with women." It was manipulation at its best, but what else can a person do when he's outnumbered four to one and he's about to be wheeled off to surgery?

"Okay," I relented in exasperation, "I hear you. We'll get the dog, but I'm not taking care of him; he's yours—and he's your responsibility."

"No problem at all, Dad," the girls responded in unison. "We'll do *everything* for him." Lawanna smiled her own affirmation.

When I returned home following surgery that tiny ball of fur with beady eyes greeted me with joyful barks. He circled my chair, stood on his wobbling hind legs, and whimpered until I lifted him up and let him sit in my lap. Later he found one of my shoes, dragged it up next to my chair, climbed into the shoe, and took a nap. It seems 8-medium was the perfect size for him too.

As Nappy grew, so did our problems.

"He can't stay in the house all the time," Lawanna observed. "And he doesn't like a leash," the girls added. So two thousand dollars later, a stockade fence was built around our backyard.

In spite of all we did, that tiny dog figured a way to sneak out the gate and vanish. He roamed the neighborhood at will, moving from yard to yard and house to house without any concern about city ordinances or animal control trucks. "Search and rescue" missions became a part of our daily schedule around the McIver household.

Nappy's nomadic spirit of adventure and his love of freedom often got him into trouble. From time to time he tangled with raccoons, opossums, squirrels, and some not-so-friendly dogs in the neighborhood. That's how he got into trouble with Tokey.

Tokey, a large German schnauzer with a wiry gray coat, spiked eyebrows, and a bristled beard, belonged to Ginny and Rusty Sutton, good neighbors who lived immediately behind us. Our fenced yards were separated only by an alley. The two dogs seldom saw each other, but the shadowy images they picked up while looking through knotholes set them off. They spent a part of each day barking angry messages across the alley from behind their respective fences. This was a workable situation, in spite of the constant noise, until the day Tokey and Nappy both escaped—on the loose at the same time!

TERRIBLE TIMING

I first suspected trouble when the barking in the backyards ceased and I heard high-pitched yelps of pain coming from the side of our house—just outside the kitchen window. Lawanna looked out, raced through the house, and shouted at me, "Tokey has Nappy by the throat and won't let go! He's killing him! Do something quick!"

I had just dressed for the morning worship services at our church—fresh shirt, coat, tie, everything. I dashed to the front door and yelled at the dogs as they rolled over and over across the lawn. Tokey's jaws were locked in a vise-like grip on Nappy's throat and neck. The yelps of the French poodle grew weaker as the larger German schnauzer clamped down harder.

"Do something!" Lawanna screamed.

"What am I supposed to do?" I shouted back.

"Just do something! Anything!"

Forgetting my bad hip and recent heart surgery, I ran out the front door and chased the dogs around the yard until I stumbled and fell on my face. As I went down, I managed to grab Tokey's hind leg. Refusing to let go, I slowly—and painfully—worked my way up his body until my left hand gripped his lower jaw. He looked at me out of the corner of one wild eye and clamped down even harder. Then quickly releasing his hind leg, I grabbed his upper jaw and pried with all the strength I had. Nothing happened. We were at a stalemate but I knew that I couldn't save Nappy if I turned loose. The unexpected happened as both dogs did a flip—in unison. I hung on for my life—and Nappy's—and flipped over with them. All three of us rolled and tumbled over the yard, creating a spectacle for neighbors who had heard the commotion and had gathered on their porches and in their yards to watch.

Finally Tokey, weary from the battle and confused by my intrusion, took a breath and relaxed long enough for me to yank Nappy free. The poodle's heart was racing as he cried softly and snuggled up close to me. There was a long, ugly gash on his throat and his black curls were matted with blood and saliva mingled together. Like the one for whom he was named, the "little Frenchman" had met his own Waterloo. I patted him gently, handed him to Lawanna, and limped back into the house. Neighbor Rusty raced across the alley from his house, surveyed the situation, and circled the yard twice before he cornered and caught Tokey. He apologized for his dog's behavior, disciplined him all the way back across the alley, and locked him up again in his own yard. We called the vet and made plans for Nappy's cuts to be sewn up. I took a quick shower (again), treated my own scratches and bruises, and put on clean clothes and hurried out the door for the morning worship services.

As I backed out of the driveway Lawanna exclaimed, "You won't need your next heart stress test!"

"Why not?" I asked.

"You've just had it. And after what you've been through these last fifteen minutes, there's no way any artery to your heart could be blocked!"

I smiled wearily and headed for the church—to preach on "peace" and "love."

SHORT-LIVED TRUCE

There was a canine truce in our neighborhood. It lasted for a few hours. The dogs were too tired to do anything but sleep. But by late afternoon—just like real people—they started barking again.

A few weeks later Nappy, with a short memory and a renewed thirst for freedom, sneaked out the gate again. He wandered north from street to street, meandered across yards and alleys, and ended up at the Wes Porter residence—or more specifically, the Porter "shelter." Wes, the president of the Humane Society, and his wife Nancy, loved animals and would do anything to protect them, nurture them, and get them back to their homes safely. They immediately checked Nappy's tag and called our house.

Lawanna, thrilled to hear that our dog was alive and well, arrived at the Porters' ten minutes later and greeted Nappy with excitement. He took one look at her, turned his head, and walked off to play with Benny and the other members of the shelter menagerie. When she persisted and picked him up, he snarled and growled and kicked all the way to the car. She put him in the backseat, closed the door, and drove off. He stood on his hind legs, looking out the back window, whimpering and whining all the way home. Needless to say that was not his last visit to see Wes and Nancy, Benny, and his other friends. In a "born free" attitude, he found freedom beyond the fence and friends outside the gate.

I folded the note, glanced again at the picture of Benny, and placed both of them back in the folder. The old file cabinet was once again closed and I was left with. . . .

Memories.

The Porters and Benny have moved; so have the Suttons and Tokey. Old age with accompanying arthritis, cataracts, and strokes finally caught up with Nappy. The weathered fence now leans in fatigue and the gate creaks and sags—a silent, two-thousand-dollar reminder of the inability to keep a dog (person) with a free spirit locked up.

But a word of wisdom from Nappy, who thought he was a person and sometimes acted like one:

"If you're determined to slip out the gate and wander across dangerous streets and through the strange yards of life, it's good to know someone like Wes Porter who's willing to take you in."

And to that Benny barks, "Amen!"

Chuckholes in the Road to Heaven

"Now, young people, you jest take it easy and tell us agin what the kidnappers looked like."

"I . . . that is . . . we're not sure they *were* kidnappers," I stammered. "We just don't know what happened. The car broke down at two o'clock this morning about twenty miles from here. Nip—it was his car—said we'd thrown a rod in the engine or something. We tried to flag someone down to help us, but there wasn't much traffic moving at that hour. Finally, about three o'clock a car stopped and . . ."

"Was it the kidnappers?"

"I'm really not sure who they were," I replied in mild irritation to the tall, lanky, grandfatherly-looking man who kept asking questions about the "kidnappers." But the badge that he wore on his khaki shirt read "Sheriff," so I figured I needed to be polite and answer anything he asked. Besides, I was too tired to argue. It had been nearly thirty-six hours since I'd had any sleep and fifteen hours since I'd eaten. And this was the first time I'd ever been in Crossville, Tennessee and the first time I'd ever needed the help of a sheriff.

"Now, son, we're here to help you so go back and start at the beginning and tell us what happened."

"Well, it all started yesterday," I began, "when four of us—all students at Southwestern Seminary in Fort Worth—left after lunch to drive home to North Carolina for the Christmas holidays."

"Now, let's see," the sheriff said as he lifted a small spiral notebook from his shirt pocket, "we need to get everyones' name."

"My name is Bruce McIver," I answered, "and this young lady is Richie Harris. She's also a student at the seminary."

"Now, what's the names of the boys who were kidnapped?" the officer asked as he shifted the plug of tobacco from one jaw to the other.

Figuring by now that it was useless to argue with the well-intentioned man wearing the badge, I responded, "Nip Anderson is one of them. He owns the car and he was driving. His home is Mars Hill—twenty miles north of Asheville. The other person is Al Crawford. He's an older student from a small town near Raleigh." The word "older" slipped out because Al was about fifteen years beyond the rest of us in age. I marvelled at him because he had entered the ministry "late in life," so I thought, and was determined that he would get some seminary training at any sacrifice. I was also intrigued by the fact he was a "fun" person, and "older" people could still be happy. I was glad he was riding home with us.

"You're doing fine," the sheriff observed as he touched the pencil end to his tongue. "Now tell me what happened after the other car stopped to help you."

"When the car pulled up beside us," I continued, "Nip walked up to the passenger side, told the two men in the car that we were in trouble, and asked for a ride into Crossville to get a tow truck or some other kind of help. Al whispered to us that he didn't like the looks of the men who had stopped and he was afraid for Nip to go by himself. So he got out of our car, told Richie . . . er, Miss

Harris and me not to worry. He said they would be back as soon as possible. Then the two of them got in the car with the strangers and rode off. That was fourteen hours ago and we haven't seen or heard from them since."

BROKE, STRANDED, AND SCARED

I tried not to let my own emotions surface as I talked with the sheriff. I didn't share with him my own fears and apprehension—the discomfort I felt about being left on the side of the road with a young woman . . . the long, seemingly endless black night . . . the painfully slow rising of the sun, and the lifting of our hopes . . . the hunger and thirst we both experienced . . . the heightened anticipation every time a car topped the hill . . . the disappointment as the car sped by and vanished around the curve . . . the guessing games . . . the "what if's?" . . . Al's suspicions and concerns about the men in the other car . . . our own hesitancy in leaving the car and our belongings to look for help elsewhere and maybe missing Al and Nip when they returned . . . and . . .

My silent, rambling emotions were put on "hold" when the Sheriff asked, "And how did the two of you get to Crossville?"

"After twelve hours of waiting," I answered, "we decided we had no other alternative but to try to flag down a car. About thirty minutes later a lady stopped, offered to help, and drove us into town. We went to the first garage we saw, hired a tow truck and went back out to bring the car and our belongings here."

"That's right," the slightly-built but feisty tow truck driver interrupted. "And they owe me nineteen dollars—a dollar for every mile—and they haven't paid me a dime!" It was obvious that he was more than mildly upset. He hadn't let us out of his sight since we got to town and had even trailed us to the sheriff's office. "Sheriff, I demand that you make them pay me. I want my money NOW!"

"I told him he would get his money," I explained to the officer. "He'll get every cent of it but I don't have it on me; neither does Miss Harris. We've pooled every penny we have and we're a little short. We just brought enough with us for meals and some gasoline. We hadn't counted on the breakdown and tow truck. But I'm going to wire my father for the money as soon as we finish this conversation and he'll send it immediately. Until then this man can keep the car and our belongings locked up in his garage as collateral."

The sheriff nodded in agreement, "Sounds like a fair deal to me."

The owner of the truck started to protest, then mumbled, "Okay, but I'll be at the Western Union office later this afternoon, and I'd better have my nineteen dollars by five o'clock, or else!" He turned abruptly and stalked off toward his garage.

"NOW, ABOUT THEM KIDNAPPERS . . ."

"Don't let him worry you none," the sheriff said as he looked at us with kindly eyes. "He's jest a mite testy. I can handle him and I'm sure the money will be sent to you. Now, if you'll 'scuse me, I want to get out an all-points bulletin about those kidnappers. We'll notify every law enforcement officer in this state and in the surrounding states to be lookin' out for 'em."

Richie and I thanked him, and walked off toward . . . nowhere. We had no place to go, and we didn't know a soul. And the sheriff had convinced us that our two traveling friends had actually been kidnapped.

"How much money do you have, Richie?" I asked hopefully as we walked away.

"Let's see," she said, opening her purse and counting, "three dollars and eighty-five cents. How much do you have?"

"Two dollars and thirty-eight cents," I replied dejectedly, emptying my pockets.

In the forties, this was more than enough to get each of us home under normal circumstances, but these were anything but normal circumstances. We were in a strange town where we knew no one; we were hungry and thirsty; we were nearly three hundred miles from our own homes across the Smokey Mountains; we had a tow truck driver watching our every move; and between the two of us we didn't have enough money to do much of anything except . . .

Send a telegram to my father:

"NIP AND AL KIDNAPPED STOP WIRE FIFTY DOLLARS STOP BRUCE"

After spending two dollars on the wire, we took stock of our resources and splurged on a couple of soft drinks and some crackers. We then sat down on the courthouse steps across the street from the telegraph office and waited. . . . and waited. . . . and watched for some signal from the operator that the fifty dollars had arrived. Ten minutes before closing time, we walked back to the Western Union office, hoping our presence might speed up the process. It didn't; neither did the presence of the tow truck driver who—true to his word—had come to collect his money. The minutes gave way to seconds as the clock on the wall ticked down. Promptly at five o'clock the operator removed his traditional eye shades, adjusted some papers on his desk, flipped the cardboard sign hanging by a string in the window to "Closed," and told us all good-night. He shut the door, turned the key, and walked away.

I watched him leave with envy, wishing I could also walk away. I couldn't. The tow truck driver was in my face, demanding his money.

Two hours later darkness had settled in on the small Tennessee town. The stores had closed and the people had gone to their homes. There was no sign the sheriff or any other officers were on the streets. Richie and I were in our place—sitting on the courthouse steps . . . thinking . . wondering . . . praying . . . hoping . . . facing a second night. . . .

Stranded.

NIP AND AL, TO THE RESCUE

"Look, Bruce!" Richie shouted. "Look what's coming up the street!"

I couldn't believe my eyes. Nip and Al in a larger, newer model car were slowly cruising the streets—obviously looking for us—towing behind them our car that had broken down. We were so thrilled to see them that we didn't vent our frustrations . . . until later.

"What happened to you guys?" I demanded. "You've been gone eighteen hours!"

"The men who picked us up at two in the morning were real nice to us," Nip responded. "We asked them to let us off in Crossville so we could call my parents but they told us there was a long-distance telephone strike and no calls could be made. They were driving to Knoxville—about seventy miles from here—and offered us a ride there. We knew that our chance of getting help there was better than here in a small town," he continued. "But by the time we got to Knoxville I figured I might as well catch the train over the mountains to Asheville, get my parents' car, and drive back and tow my car home."

"How did you find the car? I asked. "Richie and I had it towed in."

"I know," Nip answered. "When we didn't find it on the highway where it broke down we started asking around town. Most everybody we talked with knew about you, the 'kidnappers,' and the car. By the way," he added, "that tow truck driver has a mean temper. Don't mess with him. I paid him nineteen dollars and that seemed to calm him down some."

I breathed a sigh of relief, turned to Al and asked, "And where have you been for the last eighteen hours?"

"Oh," he replied with a weary groan, "I had to sit in the train station in Knoxville, waiting for Nip to come back through and pick me up."

"You mean you stayed in the train station in Knoxville and left us stranded by the side of the road? I can't believe it!" I exclaimed.

"Well, you don't think I enjoyed sitting on those hard benches all that time, do you?"

"I hope you got callouses on your behind! And besides," I whispered, remembering the most painful part of being stranded by the side of the road, "train stations do have rest rooms."

Al chuckled and Nip soothed any ruffled feelings by buying Richie and me a big steak dinner before we left Crossville and headed toward the Smokies and North Carolina. I never saw the mountains that night; I slept all the way across them.

When I arrived home I explained to my father what had happened. He had received the telegram at work and had raced out of the furniture factory to wire me the money. Obviously it did not reach me in time.

"But, Son," Dad said, "There's one thing I couldn't understand."

"What's that?" I asked.

"If Nip and Al had been kidnapped, why was the ransom only fifty dollars?"

"Dad, if you had been where I have been for the last two days, you'd think a fifty-dollar ransom was too much!"

POSTSCRIPT

Nip—now Dr. J. Harold Anderson—recently retired from his teaching position at Western Carolina University. He also pastored several churches in the mountains. Richie Harris-Whaley retired after thirty years of ministry with the Baptist Sunday School Board in Nashville. We've lost contact with Al. I wish him well but confess there are days when I hope he's on the side of some lonely road. . . .

Stranded.

DISILLUSIONED!

"I'm disillusioned!" I blurted out as I stalked through the door to the private office and flopped down on the sofa. "I've never been so disillusioned in all my life!"

I was glad to find one room in the complex called "Wilshire" where I could let my hair down, be honest about my feelings, and bang out my frustrations on the table. I'm convinced preachers—especially preachers—need such a place and frankly, if more had it, there might be less banging on the pulpits on Sunday mornings!

I was also thankful to have a friend who gave me the freedom to raise my voice and vent my feelings. Roy Austin was that kind of friend. He had joined our church staff to head up our counseling ministry. With a Ph.D. in psychology, a caring heart and creative counseling skills he became a special minister in our church and in our city. And to me. I often marvelled at his patience, sitting hour by hour, day by day, listening to hurting people and keeping more confidences than any one person ought to have to carry in a lifetime. There was no question about it: this ministry was good for the church and it was good for me personally.

"I'm disillusioned!" I hissed again through clenched teeth, lowering my voice as I remembered for the first time my voice might be heard by others in the building.

"That's good," Roy answered calmly as he motioned me toward an empty chair.

Good? is that what the man said? Good? What's he trying to pull on me?

Why doesn't he say something? Did he really say, *Good?* Maybe he didn't hear me correctly."

"You didn't understand me, Roy. You have no idea the reversals and emotions I've experienced this week. I said I'm *disillusioned!*"

He sat in silence for a moment and then replied quietly, almost casually, "And I said, 'that's good.'"

That made me mad. I didn't like the relaxed way he just sat there and I didn't like the calm, unperturbed expression on his face.

ONE VACATION . . . DOWN THE DRAIN

Hasn't this man heard me? Doesn't he care about me? I thought he was my friend. All he does is sit there with his hands folded while I'm churning inside. If he's not going to bother to probe around to find out what's upset me, I'll just spit it out myself.

So I did.

I told him briefly about the vacation . . . the south Texas ranch owned by friends Tom and Jean Martin . . . Santa Gertrudis cattle, fluttering quail and graceful deer . . . rattlesnakes and wild hogs . . . sunsets and evening fires . . . quiet stirrings of the embers of friendship . . . eerie, still nights punctuated by the occasional howl of a coyote—just the kind of vacation I needed.

Then I told Roy about the telephone call—the shrill, piercing ringing of Bell's contraption that somehow found me on a fifty-section ranch.

The caller had said there was a "crisis" in the church. No, the buildings had not burned and the staff had not resigned; neither had the deacons met secretly to evaluate the pastor while he was out of town. No one was critically ill and no one had died.

But apparently someone had said something that had been misunderstood or misinterpreted. Then statements had been made, either out of context or out of ragged emotions, that were not true. Feelings had been hurt and relationships strained. Although the matter had not involved me personally, it *had* involved strategic people in the church—and that meant both the program and the fellowship of the church were threatened.

Finally the caller had said, "Now, Pastor, I know you're on vacation and I didn't want to disturb you but . . . but . . . I thought you should know . . . but please don't let this bother you too much. Tell Lawanna hello. Have a nice vacation."

Just like that. Dump the load on me, then say, "Don't let this bother you . . ." and "have a nice vacation."

I *tried*, but the whole thing had begun to "gnaw" on me. I was so keyed up, I was ready to howl in unison with the lonely coyotes in the still of the night. Finally I aborted my vacation, packed the car, and headed back to Dallas.

I told Roy Austin all this. And I told him some of the thoughts and prayers I had mumbled on the three hundred mile trip home.

"LORD, I'M TIRED!"

"Lord, I've about had it! I'm tired of being 'Daddy Rabbit' and playing 'rescuer' to people . . . tired of having to pick up pieces of broken relationships. . . . tired of a lot of 'plain old stuff'! 'Scuse me Lord but when I told You I'd preach the gospel, I thought that's what I'd be doing. I don't mind doing that, Lord, but I'm fed up having to deal with adults . . . grown-ups who sometimes act like children. And besides, Lord, after all I've done for them, they mess up my vacation. . . ."

There. I had said it. I had bared my soul. I had shared my emotions and my bruised, fragile feelings about people in general and my own ministry in particular. I had confessed anger, irritation, and doubt. I was no longer Reverend McIver or Doctor McIver or Pastor or Preacher or whatever.

I was just plain Bruce—battered, bruised, and tired. Very tired.

With a weary sigh and a helpless gesture, I said to Roy for the third time, "I'm disillusioned."

Silence.

And then with a soft, understanding hint of a smile, Roy Austin, psychologist, counselor and friend said quietly—also for the third time—"Good."

That was more than I could take. "Don't pull that 'psychology stuff' on me, Roy Austin! I know as much psychology as you do!"

Of course, I didn't. I knew it before I said it, and I knew it when I blurted out the words. But in the heat of an argument there is often the tendency to "over-kill," and that's exactly what I had done.

Roy refused to play word games with me. Instead, he did the worst thing possible as far as I was concerned: he ignored my outburst. Like a parent watching the foolishness of a child's temper tantrum, he just ignored me.

After an excruciating period of silence, he said softly but firmly, "Now that you're disillusioned, we can begin to work with reality."

NO MORE ILLUSIONS

Ouch!

In the pain of that moment there was a flicker of understanding, a crack in the door and a lifting of a burden. So much of my ministry—and my life—had been lived under illusions:

- Give your life to God and you won't ever have any problems.
- Everyone will listen to, and always understand, the words of a pastor.
- Adults will act like mature adults.
- Life can be lived without entanglements and conflicts.
- Everyone will appreciate everything done for them.

- Every vacation will go uninterrupted and no telephone will ring.
- You can get lost on a thirty-thousand acre ranch.
- Only coyotes howl at night.

These illusions and a hundred more set me up for major disillusionments in life. This was not pessimism; just reality. The kind of reality that had a cross in the center of it.

I rose to leave Roy's office. "Thanks, friend," I said as I shook his hand, "you've helped me more than you can ever know."

I walked out the door, hurried down the steps hoping no one else on the staff would see me. Officially, I was still on vacation. I slipped out of the building and walked quickly to my car on the parking lot. The searing heat of the summer sun reflected off the concrete and into my face. A pang of hunger signaled that I had forgotten to eat lunch. I fumbled in my pockets for the car keys and remembered that I had left them in Roy's office. I moved stealthily back into the building only to be met by a secretary who exclaimed, "Pastor, thank goodness I caught you; you have a phone call. I think there's an emergency at the hospital."

I paused, looked down at the floor, and smiled to myself.

The ranch and the cattle and the coyotes were a thousand miles away.

I was back home again.

Back to reality.

SHOCKED!

"Guess what, Bruce?!" The fourteen-year-old junior-high student exclaimed.

"What?" I asked with a lilt in my voice, hoping to match the excitement and enthusiasm she radiated.

"My name's Vicki, and my friends and I have been telling all our friends at school today about the youth revival services at our church tonight . . . and the discussion groups . . . and the fellowship time after the service . . . and the refreshments."

"And guess what, Bruce?" she continued, hardly pausing for a second breath.

There was no time for me to respond to her second "guess what?" I really don't think she expected one, for her one-way conversation continued unabated.

"And we're telling everyone that we have the *best team* in the whole world leading us in our revival . . . and . . ."

As a first-year seminary student I was tempted for a moment to leap into the conversation and caution her about her words, "best team in the whole world." After all, I was a member of the team. And I had been cautioned again and again by my teachers and mentors that humility is a virtue for young preachers and that "pride goeth before destruction." I didn't want "destruction," whatever that meant, so at times I worked hard at being humble—so hard that I occasionally felt *proud* of the results. But on this special occasion, I didn't want to put a damper on this young girl's enthusiasm and (forgive me, Lord) I sorta liked the ring of "best team. . . ."

"Oodles and oodles of our friends are coming to the services tonight," Vicki continued with sustained enthusiasm, "and the church is gonna be packed out with kids from our school . . . and . . ."

"That's great," I interrupted. This kind of news made the long, 500-mile trip from Fort Worth to McAllen more than worth while—even if I did have to cut some classes to make it. Also I had missed a special exam in a course on Christian Ethics. But I reasoned that everybody including the professor should realize that being in a youth revival in McAllen, Texas was far more important than taking another exam in a class on ethics.

YOUTH REVIVAL, AHEAD!

Long before daybreak, four of us had stored our meager luggage in the trunk of Foy Valentine's 1937 Dodge, piled in and headed south. Foy's car was known as The Fireball of Van Zandt County, and it was appropriately nick-named. Van Zandt County was Foy's home, and "Fireball" was a not-so-subtle reminder that the old Dodge's motor constantly overheated.

But who cared! We were off to the valley of Texas—to McAllen and a youth revival. The thought never once entered our minds that we wouldn't make the trek in time for the evening service.

"Fireball" purred along faithfully on the two-lane highway. We did, however, have to stop at every third filling station to cool her down with water, and we kept our eyes open for creeks and streams where we could fill the extra bucket that we carried on the back floorboard—just in case.

We laughed and talked and sang our way through Waco, Austin, and San Antonio. We got to know each other better as we swapped stories about our backgrounds and shared dreams for the future. In all of this a bonding took place and we became a team without realizing what was happening.

Ardelle Hallock (now Clemons) had already graduated from Oklahoma University and from Southwestern Theological Seminary. To the envy of the rest of us she was now gainfully employed, working with students at Rice University and Baylor Medical School in Houston. The idea of receiving a regular check each month—regardless the size—was beyond our wildest imaginations. Ardelle's assignment for the weekend was to lead discussion groups and plan fellowships following each worship service.

Asa Couch, a graduate of Hardin-Simons University, was the designated song leader for the revival. His role was to organize and direct the youth choir, lead the congregational singing, and sing a solo when needed.

Foy and I were to share the preaching responsibilities, alternating service by service. I was delighted with this arrangement for almost everything I knew or had heard or had read could be summed up in a couple of ten-minute sermons. I needed all the help I could get.

The vast open spaces loomed before us after we left San Antonio. I stared in amazement at the miles and miles of ranches occasionally dotted with grazing herds of cattle and oil wells that pumped day and night. There was certainly nothing like this back in Siler City, North Carolina!

"Fireball," watered frequently along the route, hummed through a series of small towns with fascinating historical names—Three Rivers, George West, Alice, and Falfurrias. Finally she coughed into McAllen, the last town in Texas before crossing the Rio Grande into Mexico. There it was—the Valley—land of oranges, grapefruits, and some of the best vegetables in the world.

And . . . a whole town . . . (we thought) . . . waiting for us to lead them in a youth revival. Well, at least *one* teenager thought so.

AN UNEXPECTED GUEST

"Guess what, Bruce?" Vicki exclaimed for the third time.

"What?" I replied, returning to reality and forgetting for the moment "Fireball" and the miracle of a 500-mile day's journey through open spaces.

"I've got a special friend who has never been to a Baptist church. And she's coming tonight. And you know what, Bruce?"

How long can this go on? I thought.

"Her name is Juanita and she plays the accordion. I asked her if she will play it in the service tonight—just before you preach. She said she would."

"That sounds wonderful, Vicki," hoping the "guess what?" game was over. "Just tell her to check with me before the service so we can coordinate the music and the message."

Ten minutes before the evening service a tiny brunette carrying an accordion nearly her size was introduced proudly to me by her friend.

"I'm glad you will be playing in the services tonight," I said when I met her.

"I'm scared," Juanita replied. "This is the first time I've ever, ever been in a Baptist church."

"Don't worry. We're all your friends," I reassured her. "We're glad you're here. By the way, what song do you plan to play?"

"I thought I'd play 'Ave Maria,'" she replied with a smile. "That's my favorite."

I gulped. Personally, I like "Ave Maria." But at a Baptist revival? I knew that Asa would have the congregation and choir singing old gospel songs like "On Jordan's Stormy Banks I Stand" and "Since Jesus Came Into My Heart." I knew also that the choir would sing rousing choruses like "Christ For Me" and maybe "Do Lord; O Do Remember Me." For the life of me I couldn't see how we could fit "Ave Maria" into this mixture.

And time was running out.

"Do you play any other songs?" I asked hopefully.

"Oh, I play lots of them," Juanita answered with a smile. "I've been playing this accordion since I was nine years old."

That was my answer. So I thought.

"'Ave Maria' is beautiful, Juanita, but why don't you choose another number—just for tonight?"

"That's fine with me," she replied. "What do you want me to play?"

"Oh, you pick it out," I replied naively. And if that wasn't bad enough, I added, "I trust you completely."

THAT'S WHAT I GOT FOR TRUSTING HER

Seven-thirty. Packed house. Asa pumped us up with "On Jordan's Stormy Banks," "We're Marching to Zion," and added as a bonus "Jesus Saves." Asa, a tall student, had long arms and his hands flapped in rhythm with the music as he led. It was quite an experience and quite a spectacle!

Eight o'clock. Almost time for me to preach. And time for our special guest, the "first-timer-at-a-Baptist-revival," and her accordion number.

Her "Guess What?" friend gave her a glowing introduction. I bowed my head, pondering my sermon and trying to pray as the little girl slipped her arms through the straps of the instrument and hoisted them over her shoulders. She then placed her fingers on the keyboard, smiled, stretched the bellows, and hit the first chord.

I was startled. So was the congregation. Never had so much sound come at one time from any musical instrument. The fanfare was overwhelming. I forgot all about my sermon, looked up and leaned forward in my seat, wondering what familiar hymn or gospel song would follow those resounding opening notes. I could no longer bow my head and pray. I had to see this for myself. There she stood . . . to the right of the pulpit . . . just in front of me . . . before a capacity audience . . . weighing all of sixty-five pounds but handling that accordion like a master!

As she angled her body slightly to one side I detected a smile on her face. She had found a home in this Baptist church. There was no more fear. With greater effort than ever she played and pumped (or whatever you do to an accordion)!

I listened . . . and wondered . . . and became confused . . .

And groaned.

I had heard these notes before. Somewhere. But not in a Baptist church. Definitely not. And they weren't to be found in *any* Baptist hymnal!

And then it came to me. I groaned again.

Juanita was giving a rousing rendition of "La Cucuracha!"

Spanish for "The Cockroach!"

She ended with a flourish, looked at me with a warm, soft glow on her face and sat down. She had given the number her best.

I looked at her with my mouth half-open in amazement, managed a hint of a weak smile in return, and prayed for energy to stand. . . .

And for something—anything—to say.

And guess what?

I'm the only person in all the world who has ever preached a sermon following "The Cockroach!"

Maybe that's why I enjoy stepping on those rascals today!

12

Divine Appointments

"Please hold my calls," I said to my secretary. "I've got two sermons to prepare and I'm running out of time."

"Looks like things are on their usual schedule around here," she quipped. "But I'll do my best," she added with a smile.

Ten minutes later she tapped lightly on my door, stepped inside my study, and said in a soft voice, "I know I promised not to interrupt, but there's a man out here who wants to see you. He's from out of town and says he'll only take a few minutes. He seems very nice."

"Who is he?" I asked, realizing before the words were out that it really didn't matter. In all my years pastoring a church I had never found a good balance between an open-door policy for people and a protected time of study and sermon preparation for myself.

Without waiting for her to answer, I hurriedly rearranged the clutter on my desk, shoved a few loose items into the already-crammed drawer, and stood to greet my visitor. Instead, he hastened through the door and greeted me.

"Hi, Pastor," he said as he extended his hand. "I'm Chuck Melton from Tampa, Florida. I've been looking forward to meeting you for a long time."

I had no idea who the man was other than what he had just told me, but I was impressed by his firm handshake and warm smile. He was dressed in casual but neat clothes and his well-trimmed, tanned body looked as if it had just stepped off a beach. I quickly guessed that he was about fifty years of age.

"Sit down, Chuck," I insisted as I pointed to a chair. "It's nice to meet you."

"I bring you special greetings from my pastor, Tom Branson," he said, flashing a broad smile. "Tom's spoken often of you. Why just two months ago he mentioned you in one of his sermons. Very good sermon, by the way. He told me that whatever else I did on this trip, I had to meet you. He said you were classmates in the seminary and struggled through Greek and Hebrew courses together."

"Yes sir—Tom said Bruce McIver was about the best; and I'll tell you something," he continued with a grin and a mock confidential tone, "I think he was right." Then he chuckled out loud, released my hand, and patted me on the shoulder.

"Do sit down, Chuck," I invited again, basking in the pride of that moment and wishing that some of my deacons could have heard this stranger's words of affirmation from his pastor, Tom.

Tom? Branson? For the life of me I couldn't pull up a face to go with the name but I wasn't about to let Chuck know. *Oh well,* I mused silently, *I'll just leave it alone and later in the conversation I'll probably remember. After all, it's been a long time since I sat in Hebrew and Greek classes at the seminary.*

WINNING WAYS

"By the way," Chuck added, "before I forget it I must pass on a message from Tom. He said he wants to extend you an invitation to preach for several days in our church in Tampa. He said he'd arrange for a house on the beach for your family when you come. He wanted me to mention this to you today, but he'll be in touch with you soon to check on your availability and talk with you about some possible dates."

Availability? Heavens, I thought, *I'll cancel most anything I have on my schedule for a week like that! Lawanna and the girls will love the beach. It will be a great family vacation and with my preaching responsibilities there, most of the expenses will be covered.* I still couldn't get a face on Tom, but I was liking him better the longer Chuck and I talked.

"Now," I said warmly to my new friend as I leaned over in my chair, "what can I do for you?"

His tone changed and he answered in hesitant, measured words punctuated by pauses. "Tom suggested," he began, "that I look you up . . . since I'll be moving . . relocating . . . to Dallas."

"Move? Relocate?" I asked.

"It's a long story, Pastor, but I'll try to be brief. I hadn't intended to get into this—but . . . since you're a special friend of Tom's . . ."

My mind churned again. *Tom who?*

"It began about a year ago," he continued. "My boy . . . only boy . . . nineteen years old . . . was killed in Vietnam."

"I'm so sorry, so very sorry," I said with genuine concern.

"The sad thing is," he choked, "it was a senseless death. Strafed by our own planes as he and his platoon tried to take a hill. I think they called it 'friendly fire.' You may have read about it in the papers. The whole terrible incident got a lot of coverage back here in the States." He brushed a tear from his eye with one hand and paused to collect his emotions. There were tears in my eyes too. Words were not necessary.

"But that's behind us," Chuck said as he cleared his throat and straightened up in his chair. "We've got to get on with our lives. My daughter and I and my mother will be moving to Dallas. We'll sell our house in Tampa . . . change will be good for us . . . need to get away and start over. . . ."

"Your daughter and your mother?" I probed, trying to be as sensitive as possible.

"Yes, my wife died three months ago. Cancer . . . battled it for three years . . . before. . . ." His voice trailed off. There were more tears, and more silence.

He took out a handkerchief, wiped his eyes, blew his nose and added, "But life goes on. All of this has been a shock but we're ready to put down new roots and start over. It's important for us to locate in a good neighborhood and to find the best public school possible for my daughter. And of course we'll be looking for a new church home, but I'm not really worried about that," he added with an all-knowing smile. "After the things that Tom has said about you, I think we've already found our church—and our pastor."

"Look, friend," I responded. "You've had more on your shoulders and in your heart than any person should have to carry. I'll do everything possible to stand by you through this transition."

"Thanks," he replied as he stood, straightened his shoulders, and moved toward the door. "Your seeing me today helps more than you can know. I'm staying for a few days at the Holiday Inn on Central Expressway. I flew in early to scout out housing and schools. My mother and my daughter are driving now from Florida with some of their personal possessions. They'll be here in a couple of days. Later, when our house back there has sold, we'll make the final move. Just pray for me; that's the main thing."

I did, and then watched him walk out of the building. "Life's not fair," I said slowly to my secretary. "I haven't met anyone carrying more grief and heartache than that man. We've got to do everything we can to help him."

ANOTHER VISIT FROM CHUCK

The next day my secretary rang me and announced, "Mr. Melton from Florida is here to see you for a moment."

"By all means, send him in."

A smiling Chuck walked through the door and into my study. "Hi, Pastor," he greeted me warmly, "I was in this area of the city and thought I'd drop in and say hello to you."

"I'm delighted, Chuck. I've had you on my mind and in my prayers since yesterday. I want to help any way I can. Have a seat."

"No, Pastor, I won't take up your time. Just visiting with you yesterday was all the help I need. I slept much better last night knowing that I had found a new friend in a strange city. I just wanted to stop by for a minute and say thanks to you. Your old buddy, Tom, thanks you also."

Tom? Maybe he lived in my dorm? Or, maybe we drank coffee together between classes?

"Thanks for coming by, Chuck. Are you sure there's nothing I can do for you?"

He paused at the door, pondered for a moment, and said, "Well, I could use the name of a good attorney. I have some legal transfers that must be made. I'll also need a banker. Any suggestions?"

"I think I can help on both counts," I answered gladly. "Robert Fanning is an attorney who comes to my mind immediately. He's done some work for me personally and I'm sure he would be glad to talk with you. And Hugh Williams, the chairman of deacons, is affiliated with a large bank here in Dallas. He's actually in personnel and administration but he can guide you to the right persons to take care of your needs. I can give you several other names if. . . ."

"Those two names will be sufficient," he said as he took a piece of paper from his pocket. "Let me write them down—Fanning and Williams. This will help a lot. Thanks." And he was gone.

I had a good feeling. Helping people is at the heart of ministry—even if it interrupts sermon preparation.

On the third day the secretary rang again. "Chuck Melton just dropped by. Do you have time to see him?"

"Of course I do. Send my friend in."

"Chuck," I welcomed him, "it's so good to see you again. How are things today?"

"They're OK, I guess—but they could be better."

"What's wrong?" I asked in concern.

"I don't want to bother you," he began, "but a couple of things have happened.

MORE TRAGEDY STRIKES

"Last night after dinner at the hotel, I went down to the Schoolbook Depository where President Kennedy was shot. Three young thugs accosted me and robbed me at gunpoint while I walked around the area. They took my wallet, my money, and all my identification. They even took the watch off my wrist."

"That's terrible, Chuck," I exclaimed. "I'm so sorry it happened to you, and I'm embarrassed that it happened in our city. What are your plans? How can I help?"

"I've talked to the police and they're doing all they can. I'm paid up through tomorrow at the hotel and I've asked the highway patrol to try to find my mother and daughter who are now driving this way."

"Do you have any money at all?" I asked.

"A dollar and sixty-eight cents," he answered as he emptied his pockets."

"That won't go far in this city," I said as I looked at the single dollar bill and the few coins he placed on the desk. "But we do have an emergency fund here in the office. I can get enough out of that to pay for your meals for a couple of days. I'll also check to see if I can get the hotel to extend your credit until your mother arrives."

"No, Pastor," he protested, "you've already done too much. I'll make out . . . somehow."

"That's what friends are for, Chuck. Besides," I added with a grin, "I've got to help you because I don't want Tom to become upset with me. He might cancel his invitation for me to preach in Florida. I wouldn't like that; neither would my wife and children who are already excited about a week at the beach."

We both chuckled and I excused myself and walked down the hall toward the financial secretary's office. We made it a practice not to keep a lot of money on hand, but fortunately we found an adequate amount in the benevolent fund to take care of Chuck's food and incidental expenses for two or three days. He protested mildly but I put the money in his hand and insisted that he take it. He thanked me and moved toward the door.

"By the way," I asked innocently, "how did you get from the Holiday Inn on North Central Expressway to our church today?"

"I rode the city bus," he answered.

"Well, you're not riding the bus back. I'm going to take you in my car. Now don't argue with me; just follow me out to the parking lot and we'll be off."

"No, Pastor, you see . . . er . . . I really don't want to impose on your time and I have to go all the way to downtown Dallas to take care of some business."

"Don't argue, Chuck. I've got to go in that direction to make some visits at the hospital. Now, here's my car. Be my guest and get in."

Chuck didn't have a lot to say during the fifteen-minute drive to the heart of the city. I figured that he was worn out from the events of the night before and from the emotional drain of wondering when his mother and daughter might arrive. So we drove most of the way in silence. I stopped the car and let him out on Elm Street as he had requested. I gave him my home telephone number and told him to call me anytime he needed me. We shook hands, waved good-bye, and I was on my way to the hospital. And he was off to . . . somewhere.

CONNED BY A PRO

When I arrived back at the office two hours later there was a note on my desk: "Hugh Williams wants you to call him." I immediately dialed his number at the bank.

"Pastor," he asked, "do you know a Chuck Melton?"

"Sure do, Hugh," I answered proudly. "He's one of the finest men I've met in a long time. Why do you ask?"

"He was in our bank a couple of hours ago," Hugh replied. "He told me that you and he had spent several hours together this week and that his pastor knew you, and that Bob Fanning was his attorney. He said something about losing his credentials and then asked me to approve and initial a sizable check that he wanted to cash. Since this was out of my area of responsibility at the bank, I asked him to give me a few minutes to check on it.

When I returned, he had done a vanishing act. The secretaries said he acted strange . . . and nervous. Frankly, Pastor, the whole thing seemed phony."

I thanked Hugh for his call, stared at the dangling cord of the telephone receiver, and slowly hung it up with a sigh. As I surveyed my study and gazed at the chair Chuck had sat in—three days in a row!—I muttered a word that I had learned as a boy back in the hills of North Carolina.

It seemed the appropriate thing to do.

I never figured out how Chuck (if that was his real name) made it back from Downtown Dallas to wherever he must have parked his car near the church; I never knew if he had a mother and a daughter, or if his son was killed in Vietnam, or if his wife died; I never received an invitation to preach in Florida and my family never had that that special vacation on the beach.

I never found out who "Tom" is, or if he even exists.

I was "conned" by a "pro."

TWICE DEAD

Then there was the day when another stranger dropped by the office to ask for help. Larry Shotwell, one of our ministers, sat down to visit with him.

"How can we help?" Larry asked.

"My mother . . . my mother . . . died . . . Odessa . . ."

"Your mother died in Odessa? Odessa, Texas?"

"Yes, she died two days ago. They're holding up the funeral 'til I get there. But I'm out of money. I don't need much; just enough for a bus ticket."

"We'll do what we can," Larry responded kindly. "Could you tell me your name?"

"Name's Lee. Johnnie Lee."

"Thank you, Johnnie. Let me check on something for a moment," Larry said as he stood and moved across to another desk in the reception area. He discretely checked a large notebook where the names of those requesting help were listed. He scanned the book for a moment, closed it, and walked back across the room.

"Johnnie, I'm so sorry about your mother," Larry offered. "I've just checked and you were in here six months ago. Your mother had also died then. You've lost her twice in the same year!"

Without another word, poor Johnnie was up—and out . . . and gone.

He never came back. Apparently his mother got better.

THE STRANGER

What a wonderful surprise, I thought as I looked out my bedroom window early on Sunday morning. *Snow.* Snow in Dallas the Sunday before Christmas. It looked as if the entire city was covered with a soft powdery blanket, untouched by human footprints and unmarred by automobile tire tracks. For me it was a magnificent picture of nature at its best—a reminder of boyhood days in the hills of North Carolina. I lingered by the window, allowing the child in me to absorb the miracle of the moment, and then moved slowly downstairs to brew a cup of coffee and to look over my sermon notes for the last time.

An hour later I drove alone toward the church for the first morning worship service. The family would follow later and attend the second service. As I steered the car carefully, listening to the crunching of the snow with every turn of the wheel, I knew from experience that the number of people in church this day would be greatly reduced because of the weather conditions. There would be gaps in leadership, adjustments in schedules, and lighter offering plates. But the little boy inside me was so excited, I couldn't let these thoughts get in the way. It was Christmas. And it was snowing!

As I slowly turned into the church parking lot, I was in for a happy surprise. People moved toward the church buildings from all directions. The older folks walked carefully and gingerly, hanging on to one another while they searched for hidden sidewalks. But they grinned with every slippery step. I grinned back. The little children frolicked in the sparkling snow, giggling away any thought of caution. I stepped out of the car and waved in all directions, "Merry Christmas!" The entire parking lot came alive with laughter and excitement, "And a 'Merry Christmas' to you, Pastor!"

I smiled as I stepped into the warmth of the beautiful building, feeling deep down inside that it was going to be a good day. The sun was now shining, peeping through the low-hanging gray clouds. The landscape was beginning to sparkle as the soft, powdery snow silently melted and then froze quickly into glittering ice crystals. And surprisingly, the people were gathering. What more could a pastor in Dallas ask for on a December Sunday morning!

The celebrative, almost childlike, spirit displayed on the parking lot continued as people moved inside the sanctuary for the beginning of the worship service. Some who had not sung a note in months picked up the hymnal and sang Christmas carols with gusto. Little children looked up and smiled at their parents and parents reached down and hugged little children. There was a warmth in the service that seemed to touch every person. Happily, this generous spirit spilled over into the offering plates and they overflowed with special mission gifts to help less fortunate people. It was Christmas! Christmas for everyone, and it was written on the faces of families and friends who had gathered within the walls of our church to worship.

When I stood to preach I urged the people to remember the central theme of Christmas; more specifically, the central Person. I talked about Christ's love for all people and I underscored the humble circumstances of the Advent, His coming to us—an inn with no available room, a cattle stall, a simple manger, a young girl named "Mary" and a carpenter named "Joseph," and a handful of lowly shepherds.

Then, I shared a paragraph that I had recently read in The *Saturday Review:*

> "Last night John Elzy, watchman at the Grand Eagle Department Store, while making his rounds of the bargain basement, found the body of a man lying under a counter. He was thin to

the point of emaciation, apparently in his middle thirties, and was shabbily dressed. His pockets were empty and there were no marks of identification upon his person. Store officials believe that he was trampled in the Christmas rush and crawled under the counter for shelter. But they are unable to account for what appear to be nail wounds in hands. The police are investigating."

I concluded my sermon with a prayer, and then we sang the closing hymn:

O come, all ye faithful, joyful and triumphant,
O come ye, O come ye to Bethlehem!
Come and behold him, born the King of angels!
O come, let us adore him, O come, let us adore him,
O come, let us adore him, Christ the Lord.

The hymn was easy to sing for everyone was feeling "joyful and triumphant." After visiting briefly with members and guests, I slipped out the side door and moved quickly toward my office. Time was important. I had only fifteen minutes to catch my breath, freshen up, drink a glass of water, and then head back for the second worship service. As I turned the corner and started walking down the hall, I noticed a cluster of people gathered in front of our church library. Two Dallas police officers stood in the midst of them. My heart raced and my pace quickened as I approached the group.

THE DISTURBING VISITOR

"Is anything wrong?" I asked anxiously. "What's happening?"

One of those standing in the group responded by pointing through the large glass library window and saying, "There, Pastor. Look there."

I looked through the window into the children's reading section of the library. Seated at a table designed for little boys and girls . . . in a chair designed for little boys and girls . . . was a stranger. He appeared to be about six feet tall and about thirty years of age. He was extremely thin and his long black hair fell in matted clumps to his shoulders. His clothing was ill-fitting and tattered. The dirty brown sweater that he wore was at least two sizes too small and was held together with one remaining button. His sockless feet were covered with a pair of old-fashioned canvas tennis shoes that had no laces. Oblivious to the commotion on the other side of the glass partition, he slowly turned the pages of a children's book, looking intently at every picture.

As I silently stood in the hall and studied the stranger, I heard someone in the small group of onlookers ask, "What are we going to do, Pastor? What on earth are we going to do?"

I heard the questions but I could not respond. Silence. Words would not come.

Finally I managed to ask, "Does anybody know him? His name? Where he lives?"

"No."

"Has anyone spoken to him? Are these the only clothes he has? Doesn't he have a coat?"

"We don't know, Pastor. We've never seen him around here so we thought we ought to call the police. . . ."

One of the policemen, obviously uncomfortable with the situation, moved over next to me and whispered, "We got the call to come out here, but there's nothing we can do; he's not bothering anyone. I guess we'd better be moving on. The streets are bad, and they'll be needing us out there."

I mumbled some kind of thanks to the policemen as they walked away and tried to think of something to say to the person who kept asking, "What are we going to do with him?" Before I could frame an answer, I heard singing from the sanctuary:

> Joy to the world! the Lord is come;
> Let earth receive her King;
> Let every heart prepare Him room,
> And heav'n and nature sing
> And heav'n and nature sing. . .

I knew instantly that the second service had already begun. I was late and I was caught in a dilemma between a congregation meeting for worship and a nameless man looking at pictures in a children's book. I also wrestled with all kinds of emotions as I stared through that glass window—frustration, empathy, bewilderment, discomfort, embarrassment, and anger. I was angry that the police were called because a stranger in tattered clothes found his way into our buildings. I was angry because I kept hearing, "What are we going to do?" I was angry because I just didn't understand the question; or maybe I was angry because I *did* understand it.

While I tarried, pondering my own frustration, the young man closed the book. He then rose slowly from his seat, placed the book carefully back on the shelf and made his way out of the library. He passed in front of the little group of onlookers without a word being spoken . . . by anyone. We watched as he walked down the hall in the opposite direction from the sanctuary and the sounds of "Joy to the World." He paused at the exit door, braced himself against the cold wind, and stepped outside. He then climbed on his old rusty bicycle that he had left leaning against the shrubbery and peddled away in the snow.

He was gone.

The crisis was over and the halls were cleared. There were no more policemen.

I looked at my watch again and moved slowly toward the sanctuary. The worship service was nearly half finished. But I still had time to read the Scriptures, lead in prayer, and deliver the sermon. And I had time to tell again the story published in The *Saturday Review* about "a shabbily dressed young man . . . a stranger . . . thin . . . emaciated . . . trampled in the Christmas rush. . . ."

But this time the young man in the story had a face—for I had a strange feeling that I had just been watching him through the window of the library.

13

Exit Laughing

What you gonna do when the river overflows?
I'm gonna sit on the porch and watch her go.
What you gonna do when the hogs all drown?
I'm gonna wish I lived on higher ground.
What you gonna do when the cow floats away?
I'm gonna throw in after her a bale of hay.
What you gonna do with the water in the room?
I'm gonna sweep it out with a sedge—a broom.
What you gonna do when the cabin leaves?
I'm gonna climb the roof and straddle the eaves.
What you gonna do when your hold gives way?
I'm gonna say, "Howdy, Lord! It's Judgment Day!"

The author of the lines above is unknown, but I'm sure I've bumped into him many times along the way. There's a special sense in which he and I are brothers in asking, "What you gonna do?"

"What you gonna do" if you fail high-school English? . . . if you're not accepted into the university . . . if she says "no" . . .

if she says "yes" . . . if you don't get the job . . . if you don't get the raise . . . if you're forced to take early retirement . . . if the Social Security check doesn't arrive on time . . . if the children don't call . . . if there's a "blip" on the EKG . . . if health fails . . . if you end up living alone? What you gonna do?

People's lives can reflect better answers to this question than any combination of just words.

DOING THE GOSPEL

John and Doris Hurt had been long-time members of our church. John, a former writer for the Associated Press, was the editor of The *Baptist Standard*, a weekly news magazine for Texas Baptists with a circulation of nearly 400,000. No pastor ever had better friends and encouragers than I did in John and Doris Hurt. On many Sunday evenings after a long day of preaching and pastoral responsibilities, I found solace in their den eating Doris' homemade ice cream and listening to John say, "Now, Pastor, you worry too much. Just settle down; everything's gonna be OK." I knew deep down inside that everything *would* be OK, but in my fatigue I needed to hear someone say it. I also needed someone who would accept me right where I was . . . just as I was . . . not as "pastor" but as a friend whose ragged edges occasionally needed to be sanded and smoothed (and soothed). John and Doris did that often.

Then one day while I was recovering from a second heart surgery in a hospital in Milwaukee, I was told that John had died. My energies had been drained by the lengthy operation and all I could do in the intensive care unit was whisper—half-prayer, half-whimper—"What am I going to do? What am I going to do without my friend?"

A few weeks later, back home in Dallas, Doris visited me.

She said, "People ask me, 'What are you going to *do?*'"

Then she smiled and added, "I tell them I'm going to *do* Proverbs 3:5-6 and Philippians 4:4-7."

After Doris left I reached for my Bible to review the verses and to check my memory. I read slowly and quietly:

> Trust in the Lord with all your heart
> and lean not on your own understanding;
> in all your ways acknowledge him,
> and he will make your paths straight.
>
> Proverbs 3:5-6 NIV

> Rejoice in the Lord always. I will say it
> again: Rejoice!
> Let your gentleness be evident to all. The Lord
> is near.
> Do not be anxious about anything, but in everything,
> by prayer and petition, with thanksgiving,
> Present your requests to God. And the peace
> of God which transcends all understanding,
> will guard your hearts and minds in Christ Jesus.
>
> Philippians 4:4-7 NIV

Today, nearly seven years after our visit, I have retired as pastor of Wilshire Baptist Church. Doris has sold her house and now lives with her son and his family in Washington, D.C. far away from her friends and church here in Dallas. She has suffered a broken hip and has experienced a general deterioration in health, but not in attitude.

But if you were to ask her today, "Doris, what are you going to do?" she would undoubtedly answer with a hint of a smile, "I'm *doing it!* I've been *doing it* all along. I'm *doing* Proverbs 3:5-6 and I'm *doing* Philippians 4:4-7."

And to that I say, "Amen!"

"THE SEMINARY SHUTTLE"

"It's a miracle, Bruce; it's nothing short of a miracle," Warren Hultgren exclaimed to me as he visited our home in Dallas thirty-eight years ago.

"What's a miracle?" I asked.

"The pastor search committee of First Baptist Church, Tulsa, has interviewed me, investigated me, researched me, and they still want me to come as their new pastor."

"That's great, Warren," I chuckled. "But are you sure they know *everything* about you?"

"They have really done their homework," he replied. "In fact, I told them in our last meeting that there was one thing they had not found out about me. Then I lifted my pants leg—and showed them a mole behind my right ankle!"

"What was their reaction?"

"They loved it! And they still want me to be their pastor. Bruce, it's a miracle."

We laughed together.

That's one of the things I've always liked about Warren. He could laugh at himself, and he refused to take himself too seriously. He had a brilliant mind, a winsome personality, and an unusual gift for public speaking and preaching. There was no question in my mind: "miracle" or not, First Baptist, Tulsa, had made a good choice.

As Warren drove away, I remembered warmly the beginnings of our friendship. It was in the mid-forties just after World War II, and we were struggling young students in the seminary at Fort Worth. Like most everyone else we were poor, living a day at a time, hoping for some speaking invitation, or preaching opportunity to come our way. The challenge of preaching was real, but so was the thought of the ten or fifteen dollars that we might receive for our efforts. Ten or fifteen dollars went a long way back in those days.

When money ran out completely, as it often did, we could get a loan of a few dollars through the financial office at the seminary. A dear old man, resembling a character out of a Norman Rockwell painting, was the financial officer in charge of loans. Our visits to him became so regular that when he saw us coming he would raise his pen in a trembling hand and ask in a quivering voice, "How much today, young men?" We always managed to pay him back . . . somehow . . . just in time.

WANDA AND "MR. MCGREGGOR"

Warren's wife, Wanda, a charming, delightful person, worked at the Public Housing Administration offices in the heart of Fort

Worth. Jean, my first wife and Kathie's mother, worked in personnel at the telephone company. One cold day they were riding home on a bus called "The Seminary Shuttle." It was late in the afternoon and the bus was crowded beyond capacity with people standing in the aisle. Most of the riders were "regulars" and related in some way with the seminary, either as students, wives of students, or faculty members. Dozens of conversations buzzed throughout the rickety old bus above the growl of the engine.

"Where's Warren?" Jean asked Wanda.

"Oh, he's preaching a youth revival in Tomball near Houston. He'll be gone three days."

"How are you getting along without him, especially on these cold nights?"

"I'm managing to stay warm," Wanda said with a smile. "I'm sleeping with Mr. McGreggor."

Silence. Awful silence. Conversations stopped in mid-air, fifty heads turned, mouths fell open in disbelief, and a hundred critical, beaded eyes focused on Wanda.

In the stunned silence of that moment Wanda and Jean . . . slowly and painfully . . . realized . . .

They were the only people on that bus who knew that "Mr. McGreggor" was the Hultgrens' one-year-old, jet-black Scottish Terrier.

They gasped, reached up and rang the bell, and exited quickly at the next stop—three blocks short of their destination—and giggled all the way home.

It's been nearly fifty years since that episode on the bus. Meanwhile, Warren and I have accumulated a combined total of sixty-five years of pastoral ministry in Tulsa—and Dallas.

Yep, friend—it really *is* a miracle!

WHAT *DID* "OLD JOHN" SAY?

Several years ago I slipped into the chapel of a funeral home on the outskirts of Dallas. The mother of one of our members had died and I wanted to pay my respects by attending the memorial service. I was late so I sat on the back row.

Someone sang a couple of traditional hymns and the minister stood to speak. With poise and dignity he began his message. He quoted from memory several passages of Scripture and threw in a couple of moving poems. His timing was perfect and I listened and watched in fascination. There was no question about it; this pastor was good—real good.

He's really on a roll, I thought. *I'd give anything to be able to speak like that at a funeral—or anywhere else!*

By now, he had moved with ease through the comforting passages in the Psalms and had quoted from memory a portion of the often-used words of Jesus to His disciples: "Do not let your hearts be troubled. Trust in God; trust also in me" (John 14:1 NIV).

From my perfect observation point on the back row, I marveled at what I was hearing. This was a funeral worth attending!

The minister moved on to Revelation, the last book in the Bible, written by John while he was in prison on the island of Patmos. "I can see old John now," the minister resounded in a clear voice, "I can see old John now, on the isle of Patmos, looking out from that dungeon cell . . . into yon distant horizon . . . and saying . . ."

He paused, and I sat on the edge of my seat, waiting with great anticipation to hear what it was John said.

Nothing.

WAITING . . . FOR OLD JOHN'S ANSWER

The minister cleared his voice, shuffled slightly, and moved on—only now he wasn't on the isle of Patmos. He was somewhere back in the Gospels, recounting another of the teachings of Jesus. This continued for a couple of minutes. Then this eloquent speaker took us right back to the isle of Patmos, with John.

"I can see old John now, on the isle of Patmos, looking out from that dungeon cell, into you distant horizon . . . and saying. . . ."

Another pause, another shuffle, another clearing of the throat. We were now back in Psalms and he was quoting the twenty-third chapter. For another couple of minutes he talked about sheep, shepherds, and green pastures.

Then he gripped the pulpit suddenly, cleared his voice for the third time, and said, "I can see old John now, on the isle of Patmos, looking out from that dungeon cell, into yon distant horizon . . . and saying . . ."

He paused and looked blankly at the mourners.

By now, I wanted to help him. Badly. *Say anything*, I thought. *Make something up! Say God loves you, or peace unto you . . . or have faith . . . anything! Just say something!*

Not a word. He just stood there while the audience waited . . . and waited.

Finally, he breathed and whimpered through a frozen smile, "Folks, I guess you've figured out by now that I . . . can't remember *what* John said!"

The audience sat stunned for a moment. Then one or two family members chuckled softly. They were joined by others and people chuckled out loud. Finally, the sounds of laughter resounded throughout the chapel.

I watched the minister and agonized for him . . . until I saw his frozen smile melt and heard him join the others—the family too—in laughter.

The mother was buried.

Life went on.

But we still don't know what it was that "old John" said back there on the isle of Patmos.

QUICK! SHARPEN A PENCIL!

During the years I served as pastor of Wilshire, I conducted hundreds of funeral services. My goal in each was to be brief, helpful, and if possible hopeful. On some occasions when I wasn't certain I was on safe ground, I would read from the individual's personal Bible. I often found that underlined scriptures and marginal notes in the person's own handwriting were helpful in both preparing and presenting my memorial service message. Of course, I always had the permission of family members—after someone had discreetly checked to make sure that no big bills had been stashed away in the middle of Leviticus or Ecclesiastes!

One day I received word that Dorothy Black, a member of Wilshire, was in the hospital and facing serious surgery. Dorothy was one of my favorite people—charming and gracious.

As I left for the hospital to visit her, I remembered with gratitude her words of encouragement, her positive attitude, her sense of humor: *Lord,* I thought, *give us more people like her!*

I parked the car, entered the hospital, and headed straight for her room. Characteristically, she greeted me with a smile.

"You didn't need to come, Pastor," she chided mildly.

"But I wanted to visit with you and the family before surgery," I replied. Then I looked around and noticed that she was alone—which surprised me. "By the way, where *is* the family?"

"Well, my daughters were with me until a few minutes ago . . . but I sent them to my home."

"Sent them to your home?"

"Yes," she continued with an impish smile, "I told them to get out of here, get over to my house, find my Bible, and start marking it up like crazy because if I die, Bruce won't know what to say about me!"

Needless to say, I cracked up over that one.

That was twelve years ago. Dorothy came through the surgery beautifully . . . and she's still smiling.

LAST LAUGHS

If, as Shakespeare wrote, "all the world's a stage," then thank God for one-liners—for without them where would any of us be in those moments when words fail us and something—anything—must be said in order for the "show to go on?" I love it when I hear a good one-liner. Here are some I love best:

"We cannot love anybody with whom we never laugh."
—Agnes Repplier

"Laugh at yourself first, before anyone else can."
—Elsa Maxwell

"With a fearful strain that is on me day and night, if I did not laugh, I should die."
—Abraham Lincoln

"If you're not allowed to laugh in heaven, I don't want to go there."
—Martin Luther

"You don't stop laughing because you grow old; you grow old because you stop laughing."
—Michael Prichard

"Humor is the hook on which we hang our memories."
—Carl Singer

"Laughter is the hand of God on the shoulder of a troubled world."
—Grady Nutt

"A cheerful heart is good medicine."
—Proverbs 17:22 NIV

"Laughter is like a diaper change. It's not a permanent solution—just something that makes life tolerable."
—Anonymous

"I made the joyous discovery that ten minutes of genuine belly laughter had an anesthetic effect and would give me at least two hours of pain-free sleep."
—Norman Cousins, in *Anatomy of an Illness* (New York, NY: Bantam Books)

"I cried until I laughed."
—Anonymous

"Where there is no laughter, and where there are no tears, not much is happening."
—Anonymous

I have long maintained that if Jesus wept, He also laughed. I sometimes like to recall the words of Rufus Jones, a preacher of another generation. When a pious old lady approached him after one of his sermons—laced liberally with humor—she scowled and asked, "Now really, Revered Jones, do you think Jesus laughed?"

"I don't know lady," the Reverend replied. "But He sure fixed me up so I could!"

Enjoy life. Live it to the fullest. Keep laughing—and don't accept any invitations to ride in hearses—that is, *unless you're riding up front!*

About the Author

BRUCE MCIVER is a graduate of Mars Hill College, Baylor University, and Southwestern Baptist Theological Seminary. A native of North Carolina, he grew up listening to stories. Storytelling was a way of life and a recognized form of entertainment.

During his early years of ministry he taught and worked with students at Southwest Texas State University, San Marcos, and at Texas Tech in Lubbock. For thirty years he pastored Wilshire Baptist Church, a dynamic church located in the heart of Dallas. Now retired, he remains active as a member at Wilshire and is in demand as a leader of conferences and seminars. He spends his time speaking, preaching, and writing—telling some of those stories he grew to love.

Although he has spent most of his life and ministry in a busy metropolitan area, his boyhood roots are recalled from time to time in the pages of his first two books—*Grinsights* and *Stories I Couldn't Tell While I Was a Pastor*.

The author and his wife, Lawanna, live in Dallas and are the parents of three daughters. They have three grandchildren.

